WHO PAYS?

NAVIGATING LOVE AND MONEY

NICOLE N. MIDDENDORF, CDFA

ISBN: 978-1-4834-9914-7 (hc)
ISBN: 978-1-4834-9913-0 (e)

Library of Congress Control Number: 2019904921

Lulu Publishing Services rev. date: 07/23/2019

Contents

Acknowledgments

Thank you to Billy Whalen for giving me the idea to write a book on dating and money. You are a true inspiration. I feel blessed to call you my friend.

Thank you to Will Deforte for your excellent writing and editing help. You helped me take this project to the next level and pushed me to be the best I can be. Thank you for your magic.

Thank you, Mom and Dad. You raised me with great values, beliefs, and unbelievable determination and drive.

Thank you to everyone I work with at our office. I feel so blessed to have such a great family.

Thank you to our clients who allow us to help you achieve your goals and dreams. Without you, none of this would be possible.

Thank you to everyone who helped out by responding to the surveys we used to collect answers for the research in this book. Thank you for sharing your stories and for being willing to laugh and cry with us. You truly were an inspiration.

Last but not least, my two precious angels, Parker and Gabrielle, thank you for being you. You both know that with a little hard work, you can achieve whatever you put your minds to.

Introduction

Not long ago, I was at an event navigating a very crowded room full of chatter, when it was casually brought up that I was working on my fifth book. When I mentioned it would be a book about money and dating, the wide-eyed and open-mouthed looks that followed were priceless! Amidst the sea of people, someone gave me a funny look and yelled out, "Is it about kissing frogs?" The entire crowd erupted with laughter, as did I. My immediate impulse was to correct this misinterpretation of the subject matter, but instead, I paused for a moment and said, "I've kissed many frogs, so I guess it is!" More laughter followed.

We've all had our fair share of kissing a frog rather than a prince. The dating world is full of them, both male and female.

I really needed to ask myself, "Am I truly ready to start handing out dating and money advice to my fellow women?" Here I was, divorced and raising two children, with so few years of postmarital dating experience under my belt. Who was I to write a book on dating and money? What had I learned from my own experiences that might help others?

After a lot of reflection and consideration, I realized I had dedicated years of my life to helping couples with their finances, a subject intimately tied to the success and failure of relationships. This put me in a unique position with perspective and insight born out of true experience. It was clear to me that I indeed did have many years of experience giving advice and insight on how to be successful with money and relationships.

The fact is that I'd put my postmarital life together the same way I had put my career together. A creative, organized planner at heart, I've mapped out my career trajectory for the next one, five, ten, and twenty years. As an incredibly focused and analytical person, I attacked my new dating life by gathering facts, evaluating them, and creating a thorough plan of action. I hadn't been able to see this clearly until a dear friend made this astute observation about my life—and then proposed the ingenious idea of sharing what I had learned by writing this book. Romance is an obvious key part of a successful relationship, but as it is with protecting our hearts, we need to consider the financial implications of dating, cohabiting with a partner, and marriage.

A trusted friend of many years reassured me that I had valuable observations to share. He opened my eyes to the notion that relationships can damage people's pocketbooks far more than economic recessions and that few adults know how to avoid the financial pitfalls inherent to courtship. I had navigated through a destructive divorce—along with the minefield of postmarital dating—and come out on top. I was happy, centered, and running my life exactly how I wanted to.

Over the past few decades of working as a wealth advisor, I often served as a makeshift therapist to couples as they disagreed with each other over money matters. The vast majority of this marital strife could have been avoided rather than becoming fuel to the flames that ended many a relationship.

I've seen wives accuse their husbands of controlling their actions through financial restrictions, and husbands disrespect their wives with accusations of careless spending. I've listened to women who complain about men who spend too much and men who complain that women spend too much. The fact is that we both often spend too much money, and we are driven to spend it on different things. Learning your partner's financial language is as important as knowing your partner's and your own love language.

I've sat with single female clients—many postdivorce—who feel utterly overwhelmed at the prospect of managing their finances, careers, and love lives simultaneously. My friend pointed out that many women attempting to paddle their way through the dating pool could benefit from help from a financial professional.

Those insights did not come easy—or without a price. I spent a long time feeling stuck, spinning my proverbial wheels, with no definitive direction going forward. Healing from the wounds of my marriage, as well as the tolls of my divorce, took time. I've witnessed the fallout from too many individuals not taking the proper time to heal from relationships, which left them feeling broken emotionally and financially.

All the articles and studies I read advised taking it slow, and I completely agree with that advice. Too many people rush into the next relationship without taking enough time to process, heal, and reevaluate. I didn't want to make that mistake myself. Relationship experts insist that for every year you are in an abusive relationship, you should not date for three months. Since my ex-husband and I were married for more than ten years, that meant no dating for thirty months. I'll do the math for you: That's about two and a half years.

A few months before I hit my two-and-a-half-year mark, my friends started telling me I needed to get out there and date, saying, "Pretend it's research!" Even though I was eager to start meeting new people, I found that advice challenging to put into action. I had been raised with a familial moral code that frowned upon divorce, which made me hesitant to dive back into dating.

In the end, or rather at the beginning of my venture into the dating pool, I had gained control of my life and knew I was embarking on the pursuit of finding a partner on my own terms. What led up to this was a journey of self-discovery. I came to understand what it took to keep a clear head when you open your heart to another person. We need to have a clear head and a solid foundation of our own as individuals to be able to deal with ghosting and all the things that happen in modern relationships in this day and age. Once you add in money, it gets even more complicated. This makes it even more important to not just wait till you are ready, but to know what it means to be ready to date again. As it is with your money, timing is everything.

After considering all of this for myself, I realized my dear friend who nudged me to incorporate my experience and knowledge into this book was onto something.

Now I feel ready to share what I have learned, experienced, and lived, both personally and through years and years of working with couples on their money issues. Within the covers of this book are my personal observations and conversations, along with research I've conducted into the topics of dating and money. I want to shatter the taboos that surround these two subjects and dig into important questions: Who should pay for a date? How do you protect yourself financially while dating? What are a few do's and don'ts of dating that relate to finances? When is the right time to discuss money with a potential partner?

In the end, I want you to feel comfortable and confident talking about financial matters with anyone, including family and potential partners. Financial tensions can destroy relationships before they even get off the ground, and this book will help you avoid those disasters while allowing you to build a strong foundation for yourself and your partner, should you decide to have one.

Some of you have chosen to spend a great deal of time cultivating rich and fulfilling careers, and while your bottom line has been in the black, your love life was left floundering in the red. Whether you have a history of failed relationships or are just trying to find your perfect match, this book will give you the tools you need to answer the most common questions we ask ourselves during the dating ritual. A few of which might include:

- Are all single guys my age *damaged goods*?
- Is my divorce going to be the kiss of death for future romance?
- Are all the good ones taken?
- Did I sacrifice the best years of my life for the almighty dollar?
- Am I going to belong to the 40–50 percent of marriages that end in divorce?[1]
- Am I destined to spend my life alone with a roomful of cats?
- Are the men I attract only after my money?

The answer to all of these questions is an honest no. Believe it or not, more and more people have put their love lives on hold in order to secure fulfilling careers. In fact, there are many potential romantic partners in the world who are looking for exactly the same things you value.

But how do you find these people? And if there are so many just like you, why haven't you found them yet?

The answers are simple. You have not put yourself in the right places with the right attitude at the right time. The same positive attitude and strategic positioning you needed to forge a successful career are crucial for finding the perfect mate. That includes being social, networking, and being willing to leave the comfort of your own home. You will not find Mr. Wonderful in your refrigerator or under your office desk. You actually

---

[1] American Psychological Association, "Research on Marriage and Divorce" http://www.apa.org/topics/divorce/, January 30, 2018.

have to go out into the world and meet people. Having the relationship you desire requires you to put yourself out there with the same enthusiasm that you unleashed on your career or raising your children.

It's also important to exercise caution and trust your gut. Dating can be an expensive and risky endeavor. Chemistry is key to a successful relationship, but so is financial protection, something that's often over-looked by a lonely heart searching for love. Leaving your assets vulnerable is dangerous—if not outright dumb. From what I've seen over the years, recovering from a broken heart is awful, but it's far easier than recovering from bankruptcy.

While we take the plunge into the good, the bad, and the ugly of dating and romance, we will also blend in the realities of preserving your financial health today and in the future. Since the vast majority of couples fight about money, we'll explore ways to be open and communicative about your financial needs and goals together. Everything you read here is designed to help you feel empowered and in control of your money so you can achieve your financial goals and dreams … with or without your ideal match.

Before we start, I want to emphasize that this book is not written exclusively for women seeking relationships with men. The lessons outlined in this book are applicable to all relationships. I respect that many women choose other women and many men choose other men as their intimate partners. I refer to men and women in this book as merely a guide. I truly believe that love does not stop at the boundaries of gender, race, or religion, and I hope the tips and advice I offer here are helpful to all readers everywhere.

1

Discovering the Real You

I went out on a date with a prospective partner who took me to an elegant restaurant for dinner. We ordered our meals, and I settled in with the hope of a fun and romantic evening. During our interaction over drinks and appetizers, I realized that although he was quite handsome, I wasn't feeling a connection with him. Sometimes you just know when you don't have chemistry with someone. Regardless, I still had hopes for a fun evening.

After a few bites of his main course, my date appeared distressed, looking like he had eaten something that did not agree with him. He abruptly motioned for our server and asked if the dish contained peanuts. The server replied, "Yes. Why?"

With panic in his voice and eyes, my date replied, "Nut allergy!"

Needless to say, my expectations for a fun evening took an unexpected turn. I ended up having to leave my dinner where it sat and rush him to the hospital in my car, since he'd ridden his motorcycle to the restaurant. I spent the remainder of the evening hunkered down in the emergency room waiting area. After what felt like countless hours, he slunk through the swinging ER doors alive but looking a little worse for the wear. I offered to drive him home. Instead, he insisted that I return him to where he'd parked his bike, so I took him back to the restaurant parking lot.

As he confidently revved his motorcycle, he announced over the roar of the engine with a boyish grin that I was welcome to follow him back to his place. Despite our lack of connection, limited time together, and his near-death experience, his libido was still intact. I was dismayed and surprised to have received such an offer, considering how awful the evening had been. Needless to say, I politely declined.

When I hopped back in my own car, something caught my eye on the passenger's seat. It was his wallet. Whether he inadvertently left it behind or planted it as an excuse to see me again, I will never know. What I do know is that we had the chemistry of poison, and the closest thing he would get to a second date would be meeting my building security guard to retrieve that wallet.

Single Sophia

***

Even if you've never had to rush a date to the ER, you've probably had a similarly catastrophic bad-date experience. The more dating singles I speak to, the more stories I hear of crazy expectations, bad decisions, and ridiculous behavior from the people they've dated.

As Single Sophia's experience demonstrates, some dates may look like Prince Charming at first but morph into hideous toads right before your eyes. Put another way, you may have to sift through a ton of dirt before you find that one shiny piece of gold.

Once when I was chatting with a single client about her dating goals, she told me it's not so much a soul mate she was seeking but a twin flame. She described him as someone who met her where she was and matched her passions with his own. I realized she was right. Most of us are searching for the missing piece of our life's puzzle. We are searching for the person who forty years from now will love us even more than the first day we met.

We all want that, whether we can admit it or not. A close friend of mine thought she had found it with her ex-husband, but she was wrong. Being wrong was disappointing and disheartening. After allowing herself a short period of self-loathing, she started talking with our girlfriends about their relationship expectations and realities to see if they'd been similarly wearing fragmented glasses that prevented them from seeing people for who they are. In short order, it became clear that her experience was a very common problem! Dozens of smart, emotionally mature, no-nonsense women I knew had sought true love, convinced themselves they'd found it, and later realized they'd been conned. I wanted to better understand how we are sometimes so embarrassingly gullible!

Realizing how common this issue was, I did what any well-educated woman in my position would do: I dug even deeper into my research. Determined to find the root cause, I focused on the salient issues surrounding both successful and unsuccessful relationships. I began to gather information and talk to people who were encountering the same problems in their dating lives. I spoke to many women who were in my position: divorced, betrayed, and struggling to determine their next steps. They told me the following:

- "Men are like taxicabs. They turn their lights on when they are available, but I never seem to be able to flag one down."
- "Love just doesn't exist for me! If you don't find love in your twenties, you'll never find it."
- "I wasn't meant to find true love."

Were they right? If not, why couldn't they find a way out of this loneliness? Why couldn't I find a way out? I knew in my heart that there was a solution, but I could not see one.

When the friend I mentioned earlier met her now ex-husband, she was sure she had finally struck gold. Because she did not truly know herself at the time, her view of him was distorted. She was seeing him through fragmented glasses. When we are confident in our own selves, we are whole. When we are whole, we can view others as they are and not how we need them to be.

There were early signs of the heartbreak and abuse that would come during their marriage, but she was blind to those signs. Later, when she discovered who she really was and became whole as an individual, she could clearly see the type of person he was. There is a reason people say, "Hindsight is twenty-twenty." Through experience, we learn.

Her husband's controlling ways and easily triggered temper was something she found herself working around. She put a lot of energy into anticipating his mood swings and trying to de-escalate his angry outbursts. She tolerated him taking it out on her, but when he started to take it out on their children, that was the last straw for her.

To protect her children and herself, she needed to end her marriage and discover who she really was. The shiny gold coin she thought she had found was, in fact, fool's gold. Painfully, she started the process of navigating what was a very messy divorce.

Her feelings of alienation and loneliness were overwhelming at times, as was the self-doubt she felt. She questioned how she could have been so blind to his true nature. Had she blown her one shot at married bliss? She often found herself looking at other couples and imagining how perfect their lives must be. She felt like a failure.

After witnessing what my friend went through and looking at my own experiences thus far, in time, I saw that "married bliss" was a real rarity. The truth is only a handful of couples have that timeless connection, that enduring love. We all know one or two blessed couples who have been married for decades and still hold each other so dearly. The way they light up around each other, you'd think they'd met a week earlier at the town fair after getting hit by Cupid's arrow. Those folks are incredibly fortunate and part of a very tiny minority. Too many couples aim for a starry-eyed forever but end up settling for friendly coexistence.

What I learned was that we all too often fall in love with the idea of being in love rather than with the person in front of us. Not knowing myself and being confident in my own skin, I ignored the reality of the type of man I was marrying. Because I wanted a fairy tale, I kept on the fragmented glasses that blurred what was in front of me.

Then I looked back to how I'd run my life before I got married and realized I had abandoned huge chunks of my identity to make the relationship work. In retrospect, I saw how important travel had been to me and how readily I'd given it up. Traveling gave me the opportunity and space to reflect on my life, where I had been, and where I wanted to go. My husband hadn't shared that passion. Because I wanted to make things work, even if it meant shoving a square peg into a round hole, after the wedding, I abandoned the urge and pushed travel as well as other adventures I truly loved to the back burner.

After my divorce, I decided to listen to my true self and honor how important travel was to me. And doing that made me understand how vital it was to be myself fully, recapture my passions, and reawaken my true identity. I began rewriting my bucket list, vowing to do the things I loved and find myself again. I was done seeing people and the world through fragmented glasses.

I made a pact with myself that I would never live another day of my life without being true to myself. Each day needed to include me being authentic, real, grounded, and happy. I came up with more than one hundred things for my revised bucket list and decided to do one every single month.

Additionally, I decided to rename it. I wasn't trying to cram things in before I *kicked the bucket.* I was embracing life from day to day, and I trademarked the Live It List™.

The Live It List™

Flying around a racetrack in the driver's seat of a fast car was close to the top of my brand-new list, so I asked a longtime friend if he'd go with me to a track in our home state of Minnesota.

He told me, in a word, "No."

"Nicole, you always put *more* than 120 percent into everything you do," he said. "And that means if you're going to do this, you should do it at a world-class speedway. Get yourself on a plane to Vegas!"

So I did, alone. While I was on the plane ride across the Midwest to Vegas, I met a man who eventually became a client while also inspiring me to get serious about my Live It List™.

My list includes simple activities like Christmas caroling and learning to sail, along with more adventurous things like flying an airplane and driving a race car, and a handful of things in the middle like dogsledding and paddle boarding. The whole point of creating this Live It List™ was to push myself to feel fulfilled and find happiness each day, to nudge myself toward adventure and joy mindfully and constantly. At the same time, I was boosting the confidence that I had once lost. I'm done wishing for happiness tomorrow. Instead, I want to focus on filling today with memorable moments that reflect my authentic self.

You may have noticed that most of the items on my Live It List™ cost money. My list includes hands-on learning experiences that require expert instruction, lots of travel, and loads of experiential adventures that don't come cheap. My list also includes free activities and experiences. When I wrote it, I wasn't looking at the cost of things. I was more focused on what would bring me joy.

Some studies show if you spend more money on experiences versus things you will be happier. I never shied away from including anything that stirred my passions just because it was costly. I consider my Live It List™ to be an investment in myself, in my happiness, and in my ability to be a committed and loving partner. (More on that shortly.) In my opinion this is money well spent since 44 percent of us feel more in control of our lives overall when we feel in control of our money situation, and 33 percent of us feel more confident when our money situation is in order.[2] I keep my finances in good shape, so I can spend my money on items from my Live It List™ whenever the spirit moves me. This is something I encourage our clients to do as well.

That said, there are hundreds of activities and experiences you can seek out, either alone or with a partner. These are just a few ideas that are either free or inexpensive:

1. Get up to watch the sunrise.
2. Go roller-skating.
3. Hike in a state park.
4. Bake your own bread.
5. Take a drop-in dance class.
6. Get a free cosmetics-counter makeover.
7. Volunteer at the animal shelter.
8. Plant a window-box herb garden.
9. Make a list of literary classics and read them one by one.
10. Go to a swanky bar and tell the bartender to make you whatever drink she/he wants.
11. Sing karaoke.
12. Have a bonfire.
13. Try hammock camping.
14. Ask your friends about their favorite movies and watch them all.
15. Try a cuisine that is *way* outside your comfort zone.
16. Interview your grandparents about their lives.
17. Take an architecture tour of your home city.

---

[2] https://www.moneyhabitudes.com/financial-statistics/

18. Try on wigs to see what you'd look like with drastically different hair.
19. Go to a movie or a meal out by yourself.
20. Keep a gratitude journal.
21. Challenge yourself to see more live music.
22. Brew your own beer.
23. Go fishing.
24. Join Toastmasters to hone your public speaking skills.
25. Memorize your favorite poem.
26. Visit our website to see more! www.prosperwell.com

Doing one thing every month from my list has allowed me to step outside my comfort zone and discover my true self. It helped me regain my confidence and remember who I truly want to be. My Live It List™ has given me the opportunity to challenge and push myself in healthy, productive ways I'd been avoiding for years. It also gave me the platform to inspire others to live life to the fullest every day. Once I started to do that, I was able to reflect on my marriage with clarity from the "outside in." What I saw from this perspective was amazing.

I saw that I had been terrified of change, afraid of rocking the boat. That fear had become so strong that I let it separate me from my authentic self. I knew that in order to be truly happy, I needed to make some serious changes, but I was comfortable and relatively content, so I just stayed put. I'd gotten used to my life and opted to stay stagnant in it instead of pushing myself toward something better. The solution was painfully obvious, yet it was just out of my reach.

I know I'm not alone in this. So many of us are afraid to make meaningful changes in our lives because the status quo is comfortable, easy, and simple. Change can be hard to face. We feel at peace with our misery or numb to it. Years of compromise and latent frustrations box us into cozy little prison cells where we are our own wardens.

Once I saw clearly how much of myself I'd suppressed or abandoned in the course of my marriage, I also saw the reason I was having trouble finding love *after* my marriage. I had become so used to a mind-set of submission and acquiescence, I'd become a watered-down, miserable version of myself. I wasn't investing time or money in my own interests and passions. How could I ever find anyone worthwhile when I was so unhappy? Who in their right mind would want anything to do with me? Why would anyone bother trying to demolish my self-built prison? Eventually, I saw that I couldn't find anyone worthwhile in that condition, and nobody worthwhile would want to be with me.

Please understand and remember that "worthwhile" is a key word here. Although some men might be drawn to a woman who feels helpless and despondent, those men rarely have our best interests at heart. We want to avoid people who are destructive or predatory in nature.

If you find yourself struggling to meet *anyone at all*—much less someone with the capacity to be your "twin flame"—your first course of action is personal change. This change must come from within, and you must accept the fact that it is wholly necessary. Without it, you will not be able to live your life and thrive. You'll merely survive.

Your Live It List™

What would you put on your own Live It List™? Would you see more stage plays? Go back to school to study a subject you've always found fascinating? Try skydiving? Take a burlesque class? What activities do you want to bring into your life to help you appreciate it every day, and understand your true self better?

List at least twelve of them here!

1. _____

2. _____

3. _____

4. _____

5. _____

6. _____

7. _____

8. _____

9. _____

10. _____

11. _____

12. _____

Just as I did, don't allow yourself to omit anything due to cost. If you want to include "sail around the world," or "own a Lamborghini," then write it down! Remember, your Live It List™ is your list. It is an investment in yourself. Committing to the things on it will prove that you value your own dreams and truly want to enjoy your life to the fullest. You don't have to be able to afford everything on this list today. In fact, including a few pie-in-the-sky items may help drive your savings goals! You could even attach "do-by" dates to individual list items and motivate yourself to save aggressively so you can check those items off your list slowly but steadily. Add everything that calls to you, no matter the expense.

Learn to Love, Love to Learn

Change can be scary, I know, but it's also the path to growth. Embracing my Live It List™ helped me regain confidence, understand myself more fully, and learn to love myself exactly as I am. I grew so much just by making myself tackle one list item every month! It led to a deep level of self-discovery as well as connecting with my authentic self. By being true to myself and honoring my passions, I found myself also feeling ready to bring a partner into my life.

It can do the same for you too.

If your Live It List™ includes exploring a new bookstore each month, do it. We know we will get the same result if we do the same thing. If we want a different result, we need to do something different.

Creating space and time for yourself has a magical way of creating time and space for you to find a partner. You might find yourself at a recently opened bookstore scanning for the latest book by Stephen King when you happen to cross paths with a tall, handsome stranger who also shares a love of Stephen King. Next thing you know, you are enjoying a cup of coffee together as the chemistry flies and a connection is born.

When you open yourself to new opportunities and learn to love and accept yourself, you give others the chance to love and accept you as well. When you focus on what brings you joy, you will find more joy—or maybe even a tall, handsome stranger to discuss Stephen King plot twists with.

As you do this, remind yourself not to settle. Women have a tendency to sell ourselves short when we're looking for partners. We'll accept a guy who isn't quite as smart or attractive, or emotionally mature as we *really* want because we are afraid this could be as good as it gets. Settling because we feel selfish for thinking we should have or could have more is more common with women than men. Most men tend to hold out for exactly what they want. They know that when they find their match, one plus one will suddenly equal one thousand, and they're willing to wait for that magical math to come into their lives. I want to encourage women to be more confident and less willing to settle. You deserve exactly what you want, not something that comes close. Have faith that you can and will find someone absolutely phenomenal to share your life and love with. It all starts with first discovering who you are, what you want, and what brings you joy.

Let Go of the Baggage

Once you've committed to embracing your interests and passions, you're ready to start emotionally preparing yourself for real and lasting love. To make this possible, one of the first things you need to do is let go of all the emotional and financial baggage from your past.

Some of us carry compact little handbags, and others need giant suitcases to lug it all around. Regardless of how much you carry, get rid of it! The truth is that it has never helped you or protected you from anything. In fact, it almost always does more harm than good.

How many times have you reacted to your significant other in a way that was more appropriate for someone from your past? When a person in your present triggers an emotion rooted in the past, you need to focus your energy on being in the moment and behaving with integrity. Otherwise, you're asking the people you love to dwell in that unhappy past with you.

Plain and simple, baggage is destructive. Baggage also encourages repetitive behavior and enables bad habits. How many women do you know who gravitate toward men *just like* the ones who've treated them horribly in past relationships? When you leave your baggage behind, you can break free of those unhealthy patterns.

Let go of any anger you are holding onto from past relationships and toss away any baggage. Those people and those experiences are in the past. You will learn, grow, and blossom from them. You are no longer rooted in them. Negative thoughts and actions won't help you. They only hold you back. Focus on what you want and not on what you don't want. When you do, you get more of what you want.

Taking ownership of who you are and where you are going is incredibly freeing and powerful. As long as you continue to blame a person or situation in your past for your life today, it will continue to dictate your tomorrow.

Here are some actions you can take to kick-start the process of releasing your baggage:

- Identify your love life "types" (the bad boy, the misunderstood genius, the fixer-upper, etc). and think about why you're drawn to them.
- Perform some sort of personal ritual of "letting go" to cast it all out for good. For instance, you could write out any negative thoughts in a letter to your ex and burn the letter in the fireplace.
- Run your credit report.
- Take an assessment to gauge your current financial stability and standing.
- List three things you would like to change with your money and make a plan to implement them.
- Start a savings or investment account. Doing so will build your independence and confidence!
- Host a "farewell party" with close friends to cast out the old and ring in the new.
- Write about your biggest heartbreaks and identify the fears that they've triggered in you.
- Physically purge your space of old or negative emotions by cleaning out your closet, painting, or rearranging your furniture.
- Work on your Live It List™!

Put Your Negative Outlook in the Dustbin

Now that we have permanently stowed our baggage, it is time to say good-bye to any negative thoughts. Harboring a negative attitude is toxic, and doing so can make those thoughts come to fruition. If you want to allow love to flow into your life, you need to purge the poison first.

What you give to the world gets reflected back at you, which means that attitude is everything. Think about how you run your company or perform in your position. How could you have been successful in the professional world if you clung to negative thoughts and attitudes? How much would you have achieved if you'd harbored thoughts like "I will never get into college," "That company will never hire me," "I'll never lose weight," or "I could never start my own business!" You must approach your love life with the same positive attitude you use in your career. In fact, you must give everything that is worthwhile in your life the same positive attitude and the same chance at phenomenal success.

During my research for this book, I heard men say over and over again, "There is nothing sexier than a confident woman who knows what she wants and goes after it."

When you pour positive energy into the world, the world is happy to return the favor. I know this from personal experience. Maintaining a positive attitude has made a huge impact on my life. My parents raised me with strong morals and values and taught me to always look on the bright side of things. Even in the darkest hours of my life, I could find a ray of light. A desire to remain optimistic kept me from giving up, and it connected me to untold numbers of like-minded, positivity-focused people.

If you want a loyal friend, you need to be a loyal friend. If you are seeking a quality, successful, independent partner, you need to possess those same traits. If you want a perfect ten, you need to be a perfect ten.

Once I'd taken my two-and-a-half-year hiatus from the dating pool, I dedicated myself to approaching the dating world with my trademark eagerness. I love meeting people. I love seeing what I can learn and how I can become a better person. While doing my research, going on dates, and connecting with people online, I made so many amazing connections. I have experienced and gained so many things that would have never happened if I hadn't put myself out there and focused on the positiveness I wanted in life. I learned about the best brands of running shoes to increase my performance as a runner. I discovered a new perfume that I fell in love with. I shared season tickets to sporting events. I started taking a vitamin C supplement every day. I cultivated my skills as an active listener. I realized how important my health was to me. I added and checked off numerous Live It List™ items.

Opening myself up to dating with the mind-set that it would be a constructive and enlightening set of experiences helped me appreciate every experience even more. Dating changed my life, and it can change yours too—if you focus on discovering who you are, deciding what you want, and turning those ideas into reality.

What you tell yourself over and over again becomes what you believe. What we believe becomes reality. If you constantly tell yourself you have no money, eventually you'll start to believe it. If you say you'll never find love, you'll make that come true. Put your thoughts and energy into creating what you want. Don't linger in the pool of what you don't want.

Stop seeing obstacles as reasons to throw in the towel. How you deal with adversity will shape your entire life. Train yourself to view any obstacle as a challenge, something to conquer with happy enthusiasm, or think of obstacles as learning opportunities that will enrich your life instead of detracting from it. Doing this is not as tricky as "stowing your baggage," but it requires time and understanding. Stick with it, and the rewards will be endless.

A few of my favorite techniques for banishing negative energy include:

- creating and repeating positive affirmations to build confidence.
- spending time with like-minded friends.
- building confidence by tackling new challenges and activities.
- writing down and concentrating on your personal goals.
- checking items off your Live It List™.
- speed dating (more on this in chapter 2)!
- creating an emergency fund by setting money aside each week or month (you'll sleep better at night)!
- paying off your debt (when you are debt-free, you walk taller and feel more confident)!

When you have a positive attitude, you are like a magnet for like-minded individuals. People generally want to be around others who are happy and optimistic. Try walking down the street with a smile on your face—while making eye contact with people—and see what happens. Then, try it with no smile or eye contact and see what happens. If you surround yourself with positive people you can admire, people will be drawn to you.

Invest in Yourself

Just as tackling Live It List™ items is an excellent use of your money, so is enlisting the help you need to get emotionally right with yourself. Dumping your baggage and adjusting your attitude are essential steps toward preparing your heart to recognize and accept real, lasting love, but both can also be tricky to tackle alone. If you feel you need help, don't be ashamed and don't be afraid to pay for it.

I firmly believe that just about everyone in the world could benefit from some therapy, and I also know that going into a counseling relationship with specific goals is a fantastic way to get tough internal work done rapidly. Many health care providers can help connect patients with licensed psychologists and psychiatrists through a simple phone call. If you're willing to give some parameters (like where you live, whether you'd prefer to work with a man or woman, and the issues you want to address), you can usually get a list of a half dozen therapists. *Psychology Today*'s website has a "Find a Therapist" section that covers all of the United States and much of Canada. Of course, if you're comfortable talking to friends, word of mouth is often the best way to connect with a provider who'll suit your needs.

Life coaches and relationship coaches may not dig as deep with you, but they can also be incredibly helpful in doing the prework necessary to get ready for a fulfilling dating life. Noomi.com is a professional coach directory that can help you research and vet candidates.

If you'd just rather do your internal work in private, there are countless books that can guide you through the process of releasing old pain and tweaking your outlook. I've listed some of my favorites in the Resources section in the back of this book!

Know What You Want

It's essential that you know and honor yourself if you want to find lasting love, but you also need to know what you're seeking in a partner. It can be helpful to sit down with pen and paper and make a list of what you're looking for from the people you date, how you expect them to behave, and who you'd like them to be. What personality types appeal to you and why? How ambitious do you want your partner to be? What do you want from a relationship? Do you want a friendship? Are you looking for a life partner? Do you want an "associate"? The "associate" concept is one I learned when I started dating. We all know what "friends with benefits" are. Well, with a "friend with benefits," there is some sort of connection or attachment. With "associates," there is no emotional attachment whatsoever. No expectation, no commitment, no emotions. If that's what you want and need, be honest with yourself about it and include it in your list.

Do not let anyone else dictate your needs and wants. If you feel strongly that physical attraction is important, put it on your list. Your partner is not just a partner in life but a partner in intimacy. A romantic relationship is more than a friendship. Attraction and chemistry play a large role. Attraction also takes on different forms. It is physical as well as mental.

You may have experienced a time when you met someone but didn't feel a chemistry right away, but the attraction grew over time, and you felt drawn to them. Don't let Hollywood dictate what attraction looks like for you. Not everyone looks like Brad Pitt or Julia Roberts, but the right person will draw that same level of attraction and create that chemistry of desire within you.

When my marriage was collapsing, one of the first things my therapist had me do was write down everything I wanted in a partner. I came up with twenty-nine things for my initial draft of my "Partner List." My therapist then had me highlight the items of my twenty-nine things that were nonnegotiable. This process helped me understand what I wanted, where there was wiggle room, and what my sticking points would be. When you make your own list, keep in mind that not all items on your list should be nonnegotiable. If you can't imagine spending time with a smoker, make "nonsmoker" part of that nonnegotiable subset.

A few people had strong opinions about how long my list should be. One friend maintained that it should only be three items long. Another friend thought it should be at least one hundred, because once you go beyond fifty, you're getting at the essence of what you really want!

Trust yourself to find the number that is right for you. The list should be a living document that you can add to or subtract from as your wants and needs change, which will happen naturally as you grow as a person. What you are looking for in a partner today may not be what you were looking for in a partner twenty years ago. Who you are today may not be who you were twenty years ago.

Outline your desires and be specific about them. There is a big difference between wanting a partner who will collaborate on developing a mutually agreeable budget, a partner who is financially independent, and a partner who is just plain wealthy. All three of them have their benefits and pitfalls, but it's important to know exactly which of them you're seeking and why.

Reflect on your values to set your goals. You know yourself better than anyone else does. That makes you uniquely equipped to envision and enact goals that will enrich your partnerships and your life. As you consider what you want in a partner, make sure you give some thought to your personal goals and how they'll impact any relationships.

It may seem cold or calculating to make a love-centric shopping list, but this exercise can help you clearly view the type of person you want to spend your time with. Most of us have only vague ideas about what we expect and need from our partners. Taking the time to think and write it all down can crystalize desires you've never been able to articulate before. You don't ever need to show your Partner List to anyone! (Why? If you show it to men you're interested in dating, they might try to change and adapt to meet your criteria instead of just being themselves.) Just write it for yourself and keep your list items in mind as you begin to meet and date new people.

> Shifting your mind-set will be essential to attracting great partners. Be open, be optimistic, be clear about your needs, and—most importantly—be yourself!

Your Partner List

Take some time right now to start your very own Partner List! Don't worry about putting items in order of importance, just brainstorm and jot down anything that comes to mind. You can revise and add more later on!

1. _____
2. _____
3. _____
4. _____
5. _____
6. _____
7. _____
8. _____
9. _____
10. _____
11. _____
12. _____

After you've created and refined your list, use a highlighter to emphasize the items that are nonnegotiable. If you're absolutely unwilling to compromise on dating a smoker or someone who's shorter than you, make sure those list items are the easiest ones to see!

Really getting to understand who you are as an individual is an ongoing process. As you grow, your outlook and priorities may change. As you turn over rocks, you might unearth issues that need more time to work through. Do not rush this step. Knowing yourself is the foundation of all of this.

By discovering who you really are and what you really want, you might realize that the type of partner you always thought you wanted is not the partner you truly need. This is evident if you find yourself in the same heartbreaking situation in relationship after relationship.

If you have been with multiple men who have cheated on you, you might need to consider whether or not you are attracted to the type of men who cheat. You might think you love a spontaneous bad boy, but that same bad boy might love spontaneous trips to the local bar without you, where he enjoys spontaneously hooking up with other women.

Your type might be the more conservative, quiet man, yet your previous few relationships ended because you were dying of boredom. When you truly know, accept, and like yourself, realize that your Partner List could change.

If you see a reoccurring theme in your past relationships, this could be a red flag that your type isn't the type that is best for you.

Summary

You cannot be good to anyone else until you are good to yourself. You cannot be good to yourself until you nurture what drives you. As we get older, we tend to make compromises, push off our true desires, and focus on the things that we "need" or feel that we "must" do. We don't see it at first, but when we take this path, we kill our happiness in the process. If you aren't true to yourself, you won't be able to attract anyone who loves and appreciates the real you. As a first step, you need to discover the real you. Embrace the activities and passions that bring you joy. Doing so will put you on the path of potential partners with overlapping interests. Create your own Live It List™—or simply commit to doing things you love on a regular basis.

Find ways to release your emotional baggage and cultivate a positive outlook on dating (and life)! Identify what you need and want from a partner, including nonnegotiables, and keep those needs and wants in mind as you begin to date and connect.

Words of Wisdom

Two incomplete people can't complete one another. You'll deplete one another instead. Complete yourself, then complement someone else.
—Tony A. Gaskins Jr.

2

Where and How to Meet Your Match

When I was in my twenties, a friend set me up on a blind date. We met at a bar, where he took one look at my manicured fingernails and said, "It's obvious that you come from money and have never had to work a day in your life. You should buy the drinks tonight." I paid for my own drink, walked out, and called my girlfriend to yell at her for fixing me up with him!

Danielle the Dater

***

Chapter 1 put you on the path to finding your partner in life, laughter, and love. By investing in yourself and cultivating your own passions and desires, you have lit the beacon. You've let the world know that you are here, magnificent in every way, desirable, and above all, *available*. When you pursue your own interests actively and enthusiastically, you build inner confidence. You also expose yourself to a pool of like-minded people. We will dig a little deeper into how embracing pleasurable pastimes can lead to love.

What I'd encourage you to do is think outside the box and consider all the possible ways to meet a mate. Websites such as Match, eHarmony, Christian Mingle, Plenty of Fish, JDate, Farmers Only, Bumble, and Millionaire Match have helped untold numbers of people find their partners. Others have found love by working with dating coaches or through their faith communities. Still others have relied on matchmakers such as It's Just Lunch, Successful Singles, Events and Adventures, etc. Some get assistance from professionals or friends and family members who are eager to nudge your love life along. There are dozens of ways to find potential partners. Some still find success meeting potential partners at a bar or while engaging in hobbies or activities they love.

Let's look at some methods—both traditional and modern—for meeting your ideal match.

> You too can find your soul mate, your perfect match. But first, you need to get yourself financially, physically, and emotionally healthy so the man of your dreams can find you. You need to know your own soul before you can find your soul mate.

Social Groups: A Tried-and-True Way to Connect

Cultivating your passions is essential to enriching your life and expressing your identity, and it is definitely something that can be done solo. Since you'd like it to serve the dual purpose of making your life more stimulating and connecting you with potential partners, try to explore your interests in group settings. Love to paint? Don't just buy some brushes and set up an easel in the garage! Take a painting class or book a group trip that includes painting instruction. Interested in horseback riding? Skip the one-on-one instruction and try a group class instead. Nudge yourself toward the social end of your interests. In my opinion, a social group or activity is the best way to meet people.

Of course, you might not land enticing opportunities for dates the instant you show up for guitar lessons or sailing class. Don't give up too easily. Unexpected connections may still pop up. Things sometimes happen when you least expect it. When you try too hard to force something, it generally doesn't work.

Let's say a woman named Jasmine is eager to find her soul mate, and she is willing to do the work needed to make this possible. During her inner journey to find passion and meaning, she realizes that softball has always been her favorite sport. Jasmine does a little research and finds an organized coed softball league in her town, which she then joins. At practice, she meets a lot of fantastic people, but none of the guys on her team give her any romantic attention. Nevertheless, she's excited to be making new friends and thrilled to have reconnected with a sport she's loved her entire life. She may have joined a coed league because it would connect her with eligible bachelors, but she decided to play in the first place because she truly loves the game.

Several games into the season, Jasmine meets Jacob, a third baseman from a rival team. Not only do they share a love of softball, but after a short chat, they realize they've got many other overlapping interests. Jacob feels a spark and asks Jasmine on a date.

It might not have happened how she expected, and it might've taken longer than she thought, but Jasmine still found a great guy by chasing her passions in a social way. She also rekindled an important personal interest that had been lying dormant.

So many women make the mistake of believing that love will come to them, naturally and organically, if they just wait long enough. That is the same thinking that leads people to believing they will get in shape by simply signing up to join a gym rather than actively participating in workouts. They'd be much better off taking the reins and being proactive instead of reactive. Being proactive in dating means you have to put a lot more time and energy (and sometimes money) into it. It also means that you're more likely to find someone who is truly compatible as a partner. When you meet someone special while doing things you both enjoy, you forge a connection that lasts.

It is, however, important to remember that you are not just signing up for karate or joining a bowling league to meet someone. You should be joining a team, taking an art class, or exploring an interest as a way of getting to know *yourself* better. You've probably heard that when it comes to love, things happen when you least expect them. That can be true, but it doesn't mean you don't work to set the table. You may not know when dinner will be served, but you can be ready for it. Focus on yourself and what you enjoy, and that will enable you to meet someone who shares your interests and passions. Focusing on group activities as a way to meet guys will just backfire.

Jasmine joined the softball league for fun, which has to be the focus. If she'd signed up for the sole purpose of meeting someone, she probably would've looked desperate and never attracted Jacob's attention. It's similar to when you walk into a bar with a group of friends, and the men swoon over your put-together, bright-eyed, super-confident friend. She doesn't need a man to love her because she already loves and knows herself. That formula applies to dating—you need to know and love yourself completely before someone else can see the real you. The authentic you that they will love as well.

What's Your Sign? Navigating the Bar Scene

Are there any pickup lines left that *haven't* become total clichés? It may seem like throwback to the eighties or haphazard to even consider bars as potential pools of suitors, but they still yield many love matches despite the stigma of people saying, "Oh, you met at a bar?"

My own experience with being picked up at bars is extremely limited, but I do have one great story to share. One weekend, I met one of my girl-friends at an outdoor bar. We were strategizing our respective businesses when a guy walked by our table with his shoes untied, then stopped near us to tie them. This was his pickup, a clever way to catch my attention. Odd but funny, unique, and ultimately successful. I gave him the attention he was angling for and even agreed to a date. It ended quickly and never blossomed into a true relationship. He didn't want to date anyone who had kids, and I had two. He tried to make an exception for me, but I appreciated the fact that he wanted to stand by his boundary, and so it ended. (Side note: if you have on your list that you want someone without kids, you need to know deep down inside if that is a nonnegotiable item with an inflexible boundary or decide if you could be flexible for the right person.)

What I learned from my brief encounter with this man was that getting picked up in a bar might feel contrived or cheesy, but it can also connect you to people who are bold and confident. It takes a certain amount of daring to approach someone at a bar, and that can translate into useless bravado or genuine backbone. It's up to you to figure out which!

My tips for working the bar scene like a pro include:

- Spending your time at upscale bars and outdoor patios. Save the dives for fun nights out with the girls and the sports bars for watching football with friends. Upscale bars will cost more to visit, but it'll be money well spent since they also attract classier clientele. (Again, it's an investment in yourself!)
- Go with just one girlfriend. A big group of women traveling in a pack can be intimidating!
- Know what you want and don't settle. Just because lots of guys are approaching you doesn't mean you have to be open to their invitations.
- Let your friend matchmake a little. If she can encourage a promising bachelor to make a move and approach you, she should! It worked in middle school and often works as an adult.
- Be a wing girl. If you focus on helping your friend get a date, you will be more relaxed, social, and engaging without coming across as needy. Men are often more attracted to a woman who is confident in her needs and wants rather than desperate and needy.

Blind Dates and Set-Ups

Being open to setups and blind dates can lead to some amazing connections, no doubt about it. It worked for Prince Harry and Meghan Markel. The people in your life want you to be happy, and many will bend over backward to find a great match for you, but proceed with caution here, especially when a married friend points out that you're single and her buddy is also single, so *obviously* you two should meet. Just because you're both single doesn't mean you would be a good fit.

Believe me, I know.

Years ago, a friend suggested I meet her friend for a drink. When he and I finally found a time that worked for us both and connected in person, he immediately told me this would work out great because he'd always wanted a "sugar mama." I could hardly believe someone was saying this to my face. He had our lives planned out before I even knew his full name. I was speechless.

When I told my friend, she passed it off as his sense of humor and assured me he was only kidding. I decided to trust her and give him the benefit of the doubt. The next time I saw him, I asked him point-blank about the "sugar mama" comment. He told me he wasn't kidding. He was dead serious.

And therefore, he was *not even close* to being a good partner for me.

Stay open to possibilities, but tread lightly when your friends want to set you up with someone because he has a pulse and happens to be single. If the main thing you have in common with a blind date is that you both are single, that's not the strongest grounds for a solid relationship. Or even a good reason to date. Your loved ones have the best of intentions, but it can be a good idea to quiz them before agreeing to a setup. Why is this friend of theirs such a great match for you? What do you have in common with this man? What would your friend suggest you do on your first date with this person? If the answers are thin or discouraging, feel free to pass!

Blind dates can go sideways for any number of reasons, and some have nothing to do with the friends who play matchmaker. One of my cousins got set up with a guy, and as the date wrapped up, she suddenly felt like she was trapped in a sitcom. He'd conveniently "forgotten" his wallet and literally offered to go home and get it while leaving my cousin behind as collateral! The waiter said, "We don't take hostages" and told him to pay another time. My cousin left the restaurant and immediately called her friend who'd arranged the blind date, but she pled innocent. Apparently, this guy had been a total prince in the past and had never shown signs of being manipulative. Blind dates absolutely can lead to true love, but they can also be social minefields.

No Ghosting Allowed—Be an Adult

Ghosting is the act of disappearing without any type of discussion or conclusion. You simply leave someone hanging. Have you ever hit it off with a date, you both seem to be enjoying yourselves, but the next thing you, know he isn't returning your calls or text messages? It could be he met someone else and is getting exclusive or was abducted by aliens.

Regardless of why you wish to stop seeing or communicating with someone, you should give that person the courtesy of knowing you are not interested—or were in fact abducted by aliens. Though someone may not be right for you as a partner, they are still an individual who deserves the same respect and level of communication you would like.

Ghosting or just dropping out of communication is cowardly and childish. It might be difficult to hear that someone isn't feeling a connection with you, or it may be uncomfortable for you to communicate your desire to no longer spend time with that person. The point is to be courteous and thoughtful enough to not leave people hanging.

It falls under treating others how you yourself would like to be treated. If your Partner List includes qualities like integrity, confidence, and kindness, a person who disappears without explanation, even if he reappears later, is not the match for you.

If this person doesn't have the courage to be up-front with you, how can they stand up to the stresses that life might throw your way? Your partner is your cocaptain—not your cargo. That takes integrity and an ability to communicate. It's equally important that you practice the art of communicating as well. No one likes to be left hanging.

Modern Love, Modern Dating

When online dating first became a thing, most people thought it was bizarre. The idea of meeting someone through a computer screen seemed impersonal and robotic. But, in a day and age when we can start our vehicles from our phones, if you completely discount dating websites and other modern dating practices, you're missing out. There are dozens of websites and groups that exist solely to help people find one another, and they've generated millions of life partner matches. In fact, eHarmony has devised an algorithm that identifies people who would make the happiest 25 percent of couples. They based this matching tool on research into thousands of successful marriages, only match people who have a statistically high chance of being well matched, and it's been proven to work. (Their research *also* shows that people who have core personality traits in common—like intelligence or introversion—are better matched than people who are just generally "agreeable." Important to note!) It may feel awkward at first, but don't knock modern dating until you've tried it! We live in a modern world, and online dating is part of it. This doesn't mean it has replaced the age-old chance encounter at a social event or the introduction to someone new by a friend. In today's world of dating, online dating is one of many platforms to find a partner.

I dove into online dating websites because I found it so hard to meet real, quality people the old-fashioned way with limited time. Now, I am not saying you'll meet *only* quality people on these dating websites, but they certainly give you an efficient way to eliminate anyone who is utterly incompatible with you. (If your budget allows for it, the *most* efficient way to connect with truly promising partners is by working with a matchmaker.)

My first experience was with Match. I spent about fifteen minutes on the site's app, and boom! I had my profile completed. I listed that I wanted someone who was athletic or average, a nonsmoker, over six feet tall, income over $150K, social drinker, and a few other things. I was amazed by how many men dropped out of the running for financial reasons. It's possible some men thought I was a gold digger when they viewed my profile, but the opposite was true. I simply did not want to date a guy who sucked money from me. I'd had enough of that in my past.

Match yielded a few dates, but it never connected me with anyone who really clicked. Eventually I expanded my online dating options. On MillionaireMatch.com, I met a man with whom I was quite compatible, and it happened when I least expected it. It felt like I was falling head over heels for him, but in truth, I was falling in love with the idea of someone who could take care of himself financially. It was the first time I'd been with someone who had a handle on his own money and the first time I'd been treated like a princess. Seven months later, as I got to know him more, I realized our lack of connection outweighed his ability to financially take care of himself. His fiscal acumen was so alluring at first, but his personality just wasn't a good complement to mine. At times, I second-guessed my decision to move on, but when I saw him again a year later, I knew it wasn't meant to be. I didn't want to settle for something because it was comfortable. I wanted to hold out for something that was right. He deserved his ideal match as well.

Here's what I learned from online dating:

- Many individuals don't match their carefully crafted profiles. They find ways to present themselves impeccably in writing, but they turn out to be more impressive online than they are in real life.
- A surprisingly large number of people have no idea what they want in a partner. They're fumbling around in the dark and haven't spent any time really thinking about their relationship needs.
- Lots of men and women lack confidence. Even ones who *should be* confident often aren't!
- It's worth the investment of time to get to know someone through email, phone calls, or text messages before agreeing to give them even thirty minutes of face time.
- Some individuals develop a "shopping" mentality around online dating. Perusing profiles makes them feel like they can pick and choose as if they were shopping for fruit. This can come across as being arrogant and self-absorbed.
- The algorithms that dating sites use to "match" you to other people are helpful, but they are far from foolproof!
- Many of us are too quick to move on to our next relationship and haven't taken time to work on ourselves and understand what went wrong in prior relationships.
- Many men and women are not looking for a long-term relationship that is honest and true. They're looking for one night of fun.

I'd also encourage you to check out as many dating sites as possible, both free and paid. The ones that carry monthly fees may make you hesitate, but if you think about it, that fee is also a tiny bit of insurance. Anyone who shells out sixty dollars per month for an eHarmony profile is serious about finding a partner. Those fees automatically weed out people who might just be playing the field. Yes, it can get expensive to maintain profiles on multiple sites, but again, you're putting that money toward the best chance at finding a solid match. Be smart, pick one site that you feel is the best fit for you, and focus on that one—with your time and your money. If you set up auto-pay, don't forget about it. Too many people waste their money paying for something and don't analyze their bills! (We'll talk more about the costs of dating in chapter 6.)

You will learn that different dating sites and apps focus on different things. This is why knowing yourself as well as what you are looking for in a partner is so key. A dating service like It's Just Lunch doesn't share photos before you meet. If you want to see the person first, this wouldn't be the dating platform for you. It might be if a physical attraction is lower on your list of needs and wants in a partner.

Another way to consider meeting people is speed dating. Speed dating can take the form of an organized event thrown by a dating service—or it can be something you create yourself. Develop your own speed dating structure by scheduling coffee with one person, lunch with another, and dinner with another. This may take some careful budgeting since it means multiple meals out in a single day, but the cost is often worthwhile. Speed dating gives you an incredibly efficient way to connect with large numbers of suitors in a short period, and it helps sort the true contenders from the less-optimum possible partners.

As a single mom with limited time, I would meet one guy for happy hour, a second for an early evening activity, and then one after dinner. I didn't have time to waste. If I didn't like a person, I wanted to be able to get out quickly and not feel trapped for hours. My goal was to see if someone had the potential to be my ideal match. Through my experience, I could gauge that within forty-five minutes or less.

If and when your time is limited, maximize it. You need to meet a lot of people in order to find that one diamond in the rough. Speed dating is a numbers game that puts you in front of the maximum number of men, thereby increasing your chances of encountering an ideal match. It's not for everyone since it can be overwhelming and fast-paced, but it's a fantastic tool for women who know exactly what they're looking for and exactly how to recognize it.

Summary

The simplest and potentially most rewarding way to connect with potential partners is by exploring your own interests and passions in a group setting. Go into these experiences open and ready, but don't pressure yourself or act desperate. Let it happen naturally, which will happen once you have discovered and know who you really are and what you want in life and a partner.

Bars and setups are other time-tested ways to meet people and find dates, and they can still be both fun and effective. Just be smart and true to yourself if you experiment with them.

Online dating and speed dating are incredibly efficient tools for finding suitors, and well worth experimenting with.

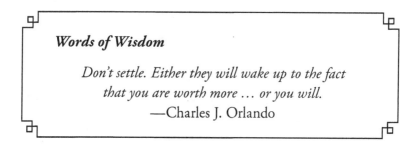

Words of Wisdom

Don't settle. Either they will wake up to the fact that you are worth more … or you will.
—Charles J. Orlando

3

Don't be a Gold Digger

I had gone on a few dates with a woman—paying for everything each time—but eventually, she made it clear that she wasn't interested in me romantically and preferred to just be friends. Honestly, it made me wonder how long she'd known we weren't a good match and whether she was just hanging out with me to get free drinks and food. Either way, I was fine with being "friend-zoned" because I thought she was a cool person.

A couple months later, we bumped into each other at an event. I asked if she felt like hitting a late-night happy hour afterward, and she agreed. We ordered some food and a couple of drinks, and when the bill came, she expected me to pay. We ultimately wound up splitting the bill, but she wasn't happy about it. We've stayed friends, but she reminded me again a few years ago of how she wasn't pleased with having to pay her share that night. I apologized, but at the same time, I thought, I am not her boyfriend and we aren't on an official date, so why should I feel obligated to pay? Yes, I invited her out for the happy hour, but she's also a grown woman with a job and her own money.

Lone Leo

***

So far, we've focused on ways to reconnect with your authentic self and determine what you're looking for in a partner, but before we dig any deeper into being a financially savvy woman in today's dating world, we need to make a pit stop.

We need to talk about gold digging. This applies to men as well as women!

> If money constantly floats to the top of your list of priorities, consider making a list of things you value that don't cost a dime. Find ways to incorporate them into your life more regularly.

As you might've guessed, I think women who chase wealthy men are a tiny bit pathetic. Yep, I said it! There's so much more to life than money, and many single women just don't see that.

On the flipside, anyone who says they don't care about money at all is *lying*. We all need money to live, and having some excess cash around can definitely ease stress. When we have more disposable income to enjoy the things we want in life, that can balance out worries and headaches elsewhere in our lives. However, there's a big misconception that money itself makes life easy. Money makes certain situations simpler, and it makes others more complex.

We still attach overwhelmingly positive emotions and judgments to wealth. Being wealthy can signify success, self-control, and ingenuity. Of course, money can be inherited too, and it may just signify genetic good luck. Money is never meaningless. It plays a role in every human being's daily life. Some of us care more about it than others, but no one—and I mean no one—is completely free of money-centric thoughts or worries.

It's important to remember that wealth is never the most significant or interesting thing about a person. A hefty bank account can't pick up the kids from soccer practice or console you when your dog dies or give you advice on your next career move. There's no denying that a man who's sitting on a small fortune has one up on a man who's flat broke, but I see far too many women—especially divorced women who've been burned before—forgetting that you don't date the wallet, you date the man.

We only need to take a look at the news to see numerous examples of how having wealth does not equate to joy or happiness. Sadly, we have lost numerous celebrities to depression. Talented, beloved individuals with near unlimited resources: Robin Williams, Anthony Bourdain, and Kate Spade to name a few.

Through my decades of experience in helping both men and women manage their money, I've discovered why some chase the wallet, not the man.

Why Women Chase Rich Men and Men Chase Rich Women

I've met and spoken with dozens of women who are quite open about their quests for sugar daddies, and I believe that most of them do it out of laziness. However, it is not the kind of laziness you might think.

Many women are more than happy to adopt an identity that others have defined for them. These women believe the stories they're fed about who they are and what they're capable of. Instead of developing any genuine self-awareness, they carry these false selves forward—many times not even aware that they exist—and let them operate right below the surface. These misconceptions impact the choices we make in relationships, business, leadership, life, and as parents.

Some common beliefs of women who lack self-awareness include:

- I have no idea what I want, and I never will.
- I should just let the man in my life take care of the hard stuff.
- I need to avoid conflict.
- I'm not enough, not deserving, and not worthy.
- I'm not capable of taking care of myself.
- The man I'm with knows better than I do.

What happens when we harbor these shortsighted misconceptions about ourselves? Instead of getting clear on how we need to grow—and doing the work necessary to make that growth possible—we cling to the idea that we are incapable and unworthy. This plays out in our relationships as passivity and settling. We seek out partners to fill our holes left by a lack of self-awareness and confidence, hoping we'll find someone to make us feel complete. Those types of relationships are unsustainable over the long haul because no one else can fill our holes for us. We need to fill them ourselves. Only we can make ourselves whole. If you are looking for a partner to make you feel complete, you are not ready for your ideal match.

In that same regard, you cannot complete someone else. Your ideal match should be a whole person as well, comfortable in their own skin. We can and do grow together. If you are reading this book, you have more than likely already been through a few relationships that didn't end well. If you want a different result, you have to do things differently. Your previous thinking and actions got you to where you are. Now we want to get you to where you want to be.

What's even sadder is that this can become a recurring pattern. If the personal work is left undone, we never become confident and strong enough to seek real partners instead of makeshift father figures. Since we haven't built a solid foundation ourselves, we need someone else to act as scaffolding to hold us up.

This is almost always the case with gold diggers. Surprisingly, few of them fit the shallow, greedy, freeloader stereotype. Many are smart, sweet women who lack self-confidence but are too unmotivated or afraid to build themselves up. They are often more comfortable letting someone else, usually a man, be in control and make all the decisions. They think money will fix everything, and instead of earning it themselves, they believe attaching themselves to wealthy men is the ideal shortcut.

The reality is there are no shortcuts in self-development. Someone else's money will never solve *your* problems. There's just no substitute for that deep, inward-looking work.

The first part of that work is understanding what money stands for in your mind.

Money Before All Else

Money itself is pretty boring. It's pieces of dull green paper, coins, or lifeless balance numbers on a bank account screen. What thrills people about money is what it gets them, what it represents, and what it leads to.

So, if you think money is more important than anything else—in life or in your relationships—take some time to understand why that might be.

Figure out what you really want. What does money represent *to you?*

Security? Status? The ability to travel far and wide? Does it mean access to exclusive or exciting experiences? Comfort? The freedom to surround yourself with beautiful things? The ability to get or do things without having to research, think, or plan? The ability to give to others or donate to causes that are important to you? Or is it really about brand names and keeping up with the neighbors? Be honest with yourself and don't leave anything out.

In most cases, we look to money to fulfill some aspect of our lives that feels lacking. We want it to fill the emptiness and somehow bolster our happiness levels. Money won't make you happy, and neither will the things it can purchase. Ask any of the multimillionaires who carry with them the same loneliness and unhappiness they had before they had money. Remember, managing money is what I do for a living. I'm on the front lines of the battle for wealth. Money does not equal happiness when you are not self-aware and whole as a person.

Once you know what you're seeking, go after it. If you equate money with security, find other ways to create a sense of stability and safety in your life. Start a slush fund, update all of your insurance policies, create an emergency plan, work on a side hustle to supplement your main income. If money has become number one on your list because it enables travel, put yourself in research mode. Sign up for airfare discount alerts, investigate home shares, plan road trips, and find other ways to see the world on a dime. If you have credit card debt, make a goal of paying it off. Or simply call your credit card company to see if they will lower your interest rate. The worst that could happen is they'll say no. If they agree to lower your interest rate, that will help you pay off your debt even faster.

You should have what you want in life. There is no question about that. However, in most cases, money isn't actually what you want. Once you know what your heart truly desires, make it happen on whatever budget you have available. Doing this will make you far happier than trying to marry a millionaire.

Build financial independence. So many women fall back on gold digging because they are overwhelmed by the idea of becoming financially stable on their own. If they've never been wealthy, they assume they could never *become* wealthy, which is just plain wrong! Chapter 10 gives an overview and case study that illustrates how to become financially savvy and use the money you make wisely. I cannot emphasize strongly enough how vital it is to work yourself into a position of total autonomy. The only way to ensure true financial security is to take care of and rely on yourself. It doesn't mean you will always need to. You need to be able to. You need to know how. If you don't, and your only plan is to attach yourself to a wealthy man, what will you do if he loses interest in you? Moves? Gets in a car accident? Dating someone rich is *not* a financial plan.

However, if you know you have some gold-digging tendencies, be honest with yourself about that. Don't push it away or pretend it's not there. That will just keep you stuck in the cycle. Instead, bring it in, own it, and figure out what's really going on.

When you do all the emotional work and still decide that being with someone who outearns you is important, at least you'll understand why. You may be someone who enjoys relinquishing control to someone else, or maybe you've reached a point in your life when you are ready to focus more on raising a family or charitable work. As long as your reasons aren't rooted in fear or a lack of confidence, and as long as you know exactly what those motivations are, you can honor them with a clean conscience. The important thing is that you have the tools and knowledge to take care of yourself and be financially independent—even if you don't need to.

What to Do if You End Up Dating a Gold Digger

That's right—this door swings both ways! There are plenty of guys out there who'd love nothing more than to land a woman in a better financial situation than they are and let her take care of them. Keep in mind you don't need to be wealthy to be the victim of a gold digger. Wealth is relative, especially in the eyes of someone looking to turn you into their meal ticket.

There are a few ways to tell if a man is an aspiring gold digger. Some red flags include asking what kind of car you drive before you've even met in person, commenting on your jewelry or the clothing brands you wear in your profile photos, constant comments about how wealthy you are or seem, and demanding to go to expensive restaurants, do expensive activities, or attend spendy sports events, all on your dime. A gold digger will ask you for money. Even if it is twenty dollars here and there—or two thousand—he should not be asking you for money. To him, the whole world revolves around money and what people have rather than who they are.

What happens if you see none of those red flags fly until you're three or four dates in? How do you handle it if you discover that someone you've been dating is only interested in your money?

Keep a clear head. If, from a financial standpoint, you're not putting yourself at risk, you get to choose. It might be worthwhile to have this man in your life if you truly enjoy his company and don't mind footing the bill for everything yourself. If you're head over heels before you realize he's a bit of a gold digger, weigh your options. Be aware of what's happening and make your choices wisely.

Make sure it's about money. Sometimes they're in it for the lifestyle more than the money. It can be hard to tell the difference, but that distinction can be important. Is he with you because you're always traveling and doing fun things together? If you continued to plan and organize those activities but asked him to pay his share, would that work? Sometimes, as the planner, you end up springing for tickets and admission fees because it's easier and more seamless than figuring out how to split costs. It could also be that you spring for the tickets before the event, and he pays for the food and parking and anything at the event. Take a step back and make sure you're actually *asking* him to pull his weight. It's a balance. That's what relationships are made of.

Keep things separate. Whatever you do, don't ever loan him money. Unfortunately, I've heard of this happening too many times. Guys hit up their new girlfriends for money, and when they do, they always say, "It's just a loan. I'll pay you back." But in all the years I've been a wealth advisor—thinking back over all the clients who trusted suitors with loaned cash—I cannot remember a single time when the guy in question paid back an off-the-books loan in full. Don't give him money. And if you just can't resist his charms and end up writing him a check, don't expect to see a dime back—no matter what he says.

Don't pay off his loans or credit cards. Don't combine finances too soon. You can counsel him and show him how to manage his own money better or help him boost his credit independently. Do so from an educational standpoint. Sometimes a man goes through a rough time. Health issues, custody or divorce costs, and unexpected home repairs happen to a lot of us. Instead of throwing cash at the issue, help him by sharing a few things you know or have learned—gently and diplomatically, of course. Guide him toward more informed decision-making without being judgmental or demeaning. If he has gold-digging tendencies, don't let your finances get intertwined.

The only way to truly help him, as you might feel you need to do, is to share knowledge with him so that he can gain financial independence while working on himself as an individual, the way you have. There is truth behind the proverb: "You give a poor man a fish and you feed him for a day. You teach him to fish, and you give him an occupation that will feed him for a lifetime."

Watch Out for Unconscious Freeloading

We tend to think of gold diggers as people who glom onto high earners for the long haul, but you don't have to squeeze a diamond ring out of a rich guy to make him feel used. Take another look at Lone Leo's story at the beginning of this chapter. Have you ever done anything similar to a guy friend you had no intention of dating? Or even to a man you were seeing, but instinctively knew wasn't "the one"?

I'd bet the vast majority of you took one look at the title of this chapter and thought, *Oh, well, that's not me!* Maybe it's not, from a big picture perspective. If you expect the men you date, wealthy or not, to fund absolutely everything all the time, you might be toeing the line a bit. Chapter 6 will explore the politics of who pays for dates in depth, but for now, suffice it to say that it's never wise or kind to take advantage of someone—no matter how big his trust fund, successful his business, or impressive his investment portfolio may be.

Summary

Gold digging, while ill-advised, is often rooted in a lack of self-confidence and self-awareness. If you find yourself believing that a rich man will solve all your problems, take a step back. Explore what money represents to you and then find other ways to fulfill those needs.

Words of Wisdom

Don't be afraid to lose him, because if a man truly loves you, he's not going anywhere.
—Steve Harvey

4

Dating Guidelines to Live By

I was a groomsman in a friend's wedding, and I really hit it off with one of the wedding guests. During the reception, she and I hung out together for the entire evening and had an amazing time. Afterward, a group of us were planning to go to a club downtown, so I invited her along. She agreed to join us. I even volunteered to pay her admission to the club. When we got to the club, I realized that I didn't have any cash on me, and they weren't taking credit cards at the door. She had to dip into her wallet to cover admission for both of us. Needless to say, she wasn't happy about this. When we got inside, she completely ignored me and decided to go do her own thing. We never spoke again.

Bachelor Brandon

***

Dating is a dance. It's not something you do alone; it's something you do with others. It might feel unnatural to look to your partner for cues about how to behave. Let him lead, let yourself follow, and watch to see how the dance unfolds. Sometimes even the best dancers step on a toe now and then.

Having said that, if you don't have a set of ground rules before you hit the dance floor, your partner can end up leading you on some serious wild goose chases (or coercing you into endless rounds of the Electric Slide). Yes, you want to be flexible and open and willing to take chances and try new things, but you also want to be levelheaded, sure of yourself, and solid in your goals. You need a personal code, you need boundaries, and you need to know how to comport yourself if a misstep occurs and your toe gets stepped on.

The Ten Commandments of Dating

With that in mind, here are what I've determined to be the Ten Commandments of Dating. I know I'm not a dating expert, but I've been single, married, divorced, and single again, so I have learned a few key things about dating, especially from a financial perspective. In my work as a wealth advisor, I've counseled countless couples through monetary minefields and steered them away from divorce and toward honest fiscal partnerships. Helping others weed through the financial issues that crop up in their relationships has taught me a ton about those times when money and love tend to clash!

These commandments came from my own experiences, from stories that clients shared, from friends and strangers, from managing money for couples all these years, from interviews with dating matchmakers, and from both experienced and inexperienced daters. I did my best to gather information and opinions from a diverse group of people. Here's what they told me:

1. Thou shall not appear desperate.
2. Thou shall not live in denial.
3. Thou shall know thine own direction in life.
4. Thou shall know thine own wants.
5. Thou shall not just text.
6. Thou shall protect thyself.
7. Thou shall set good boundaries.
8. Thou shall love thyself first.
9. Thou shall date through all four seasons.
10. Thou shall not send a plant. (Thou shall really listen to what others want.)

The purpose of every commandment will be explained in detail in the pages that follow to help you apply them—either sparingly or generously—according to your specific needs. No set of rules is foolproof, but having a solid set of guidelines to follow can help you avoid some of the most typical undesirable outcomes. Common sense should guide you the rest of the way. The golden rule of "Treat others how you would like to be treated," applies here as well.

And speaking of common sense, bear in mind that these commandments are just guidelines. All rules work best accompanied by good judgement, and that includes these! As with everything in life, too much or too little control can be disastrous. Your gut is typically your best guide, so trust your intuition as you decide how to use these commandments in your own dating life.

Thou Shall Not Appear Desperate

This may sound silly, but this commandment holds the top spot for one simple reason: Many of us have a hard time differentiating between appearing available and looking desperate. As a woman who is interested in finding a partner, you don't want to seem off-limits, cold, or disinterested. Reversely, crank that availability vibe up too high will give off signals of neediness and anxiety, which are a total turnoff. A desperate woman is like Kryptonite to a single man.

In fact, I'd go so far as to say that an overeager or playfully aggressive woman can drive away quality suitors. Even in today's environment, when it is socially acceptable for women to pursue men, I would strongly advise against doing so. "Never drink from another man's cup—always let him drink from yours." This saying holds as true today as it did when my grandmother heard it from her own mother.

Men may tell you that they find it flattering when women pursue them, but what they're not telling you is that most of the women they'd prefer to date are *the ones they pursued themselves.* Of course, there are anomalies, and many of us have heard stories to the contrary: women going after men, landing them, and living happily ever after. Even though those may be true tales, they are relatively rare events, and we are going to focus on the law of averages. In most cases, men would rather pursue the women who interest them. For a man, being pursued may feel good, but it seldom leads to lifelong love matches.

This was a lesson I learned the hard way, but once I embraced it, my dating life was transformed. I live in the Midwest where men are pretty relaxed overall, but they can be incredibly hesitant to make the first move. Yet when I was bold enough to ask a man out myself, it never came to anything! Eventually, I started dating men from the East Coast or West Coast since they tended to have enough confidence to actually approach me and ask me out.

So, just how do you appear available without looking desperate? First, you must be confident. Confidence sends the message that you are there—present and worth noticing—to everyone in the room. Your presence and poise will draw people to you. Be sure to blend those qualities with a measure of approachable social grace. Translation: Speak to everybody and listen to what they have to say. Have you ever observed a beautiful flight attendant with great social skills going about her work? She speaks with a smile and is always happy to listen to everyone who speaks to her. Every guy on the plane recognizes her openness, and every woman envies her conversational prowess. She could be married with three children at home, and you would never know it because every man on the plane wants to date her. She is funny, approachable, spunky, full of energy, and easy to like. Those are great social skills you will want to develop if you don't already have them.

Another key to broadcasting availability without seeming overeager is to push back, never letting yourself be overly agreeable at first. A new relationship is like a good stew. It's better after a long simmer. The truth is, guys like a little bit of mystery in women, so don't feel obliged to agree with everything he says or laugh at all of his jokes. Play devil's advocate, express contrary opinions, press him to explain his thinking. Of course, too much distance can cause a budding romance to die on the vine, so be careful in how you apply this advice. Bear in mind that few guys are looking for a woman who just blindly agrees with everything they say, at least not the type of man who will be a true partner.

Next, let him give you a little attention by pursuing you, and let yourself enjoy being chased. The intensity or amount of attention he gives you at this phase can be used as a barometer. The more attention he gives, the higher his level of interest in you. For example, if Tate calls you twelve times a week and asks you out twice, he is probably more interested than Damon, who calls you only three times a week. My mother once told me that even the busiest person in the world has time for the person he cares for. If someone is "too busy" for you, he probably isn't that into you. People make time for the things that are truly important to them. If a guy truly wants to date you, he will make time. We all have the same twenty-four hours in a day. You know when you are or are not someone's priority.

A rule I strongly recommend is if he calls or texts at five in the evening to see you at seven that same night, no matter how much you want to see him, say no. You never want to appear available to someone's beck and call. We train people in how we want to be treated. If a gentleman can't plan ahead for a date, how can he be the man who will create and plan a life with you?

Finally, whatever you do, do *not* call or text more than twice! He received your call or text, and he will reply if he's interested. There's no need to double-check. Unfortunately, we cannot control anyone else's schedule—even the guy we think is our knight in shining armor. We cannot force responses. Blowing up his phone with texts and voice mails will just make it seem like you've got too much time on your hands. Busy people want to spend time with other busy people, so instead of stalking him by phone, cultivate your own hobbies, activities, and commitments. Build a fulfilling life for yourself so that your soul mate will complement what you've already built. Don't rely on a partner to fill the void—and don't crush him under a giant pile of voice mail messages.

Thou Shall Not Live in Denial

It can be so easy to ignore warning signals and brush off sketchy behavior when you think you're falling for a guy. It is key that you learn to keep your head clear and your eyes open. If a man won't tell you what he does for a living, that's a major red flag. If a man acts like he might be married, he probably is. I met a guy for the first time, and he had a wedding ring on, but a few hours later, that ring was magically gone. I've also dated men who were deeply offended when I declined to send them endless photos of myself. When someone is so obsessed with sending and receiving pics, you've got to wonder, "What's their true intent?" Don't waste your time if someone you're dating sets off your internal alarms. Trust your gut and don't deny yourself. When you think something seems fishy, it usually is.

If you don't think a guy is truly interested in you, you're probably right. If he seems like he might be a user, a player, or a gold digger, listen to your instincts and walk away.

The pursuit of love can make us downright daffy, but you do *not* want to be in a foggy state of denial when you are dating. Watch for the signs, see the person in front of you, listen to your partner, and listen to yourself.

Thou Shall Know Thine Own Direction in Life

You need to know and love yourself first before you can love anyone else. I cannot emphasize this strongly enough. Have your own goals, dreams, and desires. Have your own life and your own amazing group of friends. Be financially strong and stable. You generally attract people who are playing at your level, so level up strategically and know exactly where you're going. When you're grounded and have built a great life, you'll attract other people who are grounded and have great lives. If you want to date a "perfect ten," then work to get yourself to be a "perfect ten" first. If you want a partner who's at the top of his field, drive yourself to the top of your own field. Know who you are, own your accomplishments, and look for partners who do the same.

On a related note, be sure to know your worth and avoid dating people because of their money. Life isn't all about the money. If you find yourself dating someone because you enjoy being around wealth, think long and hard about how this could work for you in the long term. Consider your core values and what is truly important to you. Usually, it isn't the money. (Head back to chapter 3 if you need more guidance on this topic.)

Thou Shall Know Thine Own Wants

Once you know who you are, figure out what you want from a relationship. Create your list of things you want in a partner—and stick to it. (We touched on this in chapter 1.) Don't feel obliged to share that list with anyone. I quickly learned *not* to share my Partner List with anyone I would potentially date. Once a guy got a look at my criteria, he did his best to start influencing my wants and convince me that he was everything I'd ever dreamed of. I stopped sharing my list and would advise you to do the same. Show it to a guy you're dating, and he may try to morph into someone who checks all the boxes. You'll be looking at him through rose-colored glasses, and your list will lose its effect. It should keep you focused on what is important to you and not encourage some guy to retrofit himself so he meets your carefully considered criteria.

Make sure you know the difference between the nonnegotiables on your list and items that have a little leeway built in. Maybe "nonsmoker" and "dog lover" are absolutes, but "close with his family" and "marathon runner" aren't as essential. April Davis, owner of LUMA Luxury Matchmaking says, "While looking for potential boyfriends, keep a middle-of-the-road mentality. If you've been burned in the past by a low-life and now you think money is the most important criteria, think again." She's got a great point: If some characteristic has proven troublesome in past boyfriends (like having no money), don't assume that going to the opposite extreme (being wealthy) will fix everything. Create parameters—not hard criteria. If you meet someone amazing who can't even be wedged into your set of parameters, let the strength of his character float to the top of the list.

When you meet someone who seems to be your perfect match—that guy who makes you feel all tingly and flustered whenever you see him—all your carefully crafted rules may go out the window. Even if he doesn't check off some very important boxes, it can be hard to overlook a strong emotional connection. Sometimes it's worth bending the rules for the right person, but be very, very careful about doing this. Many times, when you're tempted to make exceptions for someone who appears to be Mr. Right, you'll find out later that he's really Mr. Oh-So-Wrong.

Again, be reasonable when it comes to net worth and earning potential. It is, of course, totally reasonable to limit your dating partners to men who earn as much or more than you do. Both men and women typically want partners who are on fairly equal financial footing, and few are comfortable with huge income gaps, but if you're earning in the low $20Ks and insist on dating men who earn $250K or more, you need to consider your reasoning. As we will explore in the coming chapters, how much he earns is a factor, but it should not be the sole deciding factor.

Thou Shall Not Just Text

Texting definitely has its charms. It's not as intense as a phone call, but it's not as impersonal as an email. Just remember that when you text, even though you may send with a certain emotion in mind, the recipient may read other emotions into it. Just like email or any written correspondence, text messages can be misconstrued since they don't convey tone of voice and aren't accompanied by facial expressions. For these simple reasons, texting is not the best medium for a full-blown conversation and should not replace necessary face-to-face discussions. Once I received a text that said: "I think we should just be friends." I was hurt and insulted since I believe breaking up is a conversation you *always* have in person. Don't text anything that makes declarations or asks questions about the state of your relationship. Force yourself to talk about anything serious or emotionally weighty in person.

That said, texting can be very useful under certain circumstances. Before meeting for a first date, it's not a bad idea to text back and forth to get to know each other's communication styles—or if you're a single parent and getting kids to bed at night and you don't want to wake them up. Be aware that when you meet in person, a guy may be quite different than he seemed over text. I remember one week when I went on five dates and discovered that the guy who had the most amazing banter via text (and who I was most excited to meet) turned out to be the worst date. The guy who was the least interesting texter (and the one I was least excited to meet) turned out to be the best of the five. Some people are actually more comfortable at a keyboard than they are face-to-face.

If you're looking for a happy medium, consider an actual phone conversation (a groundbreaking suggestion in this text-centric world, but one worth considering)! Don't underestimate the importance of hearing someone's voice and getting a read on his emotions before meeting in person. A quick twenty-minute call may be all you need to cement your chemistry or realize you're a terrible match.

Don't let texting be the medium for truly important messages—but do employ text strategically.

Thou Shall Protect Thyself

It can be hard to tell the good guys from the bad ones at first glance, but you can do a few simple things to watch your own back. For a first date, meet in a public place with a set time limit. Make sure a friend always knows where you are. Don't give out your personal information too soon. If you get a bad feeling about someone, trust your gut and get out—politeness be damned. Your safety is more important than social graces.

It is also important to know who you are dating. Thankfully, that's pretty easy to find out with a little online sleuthing. Naturally, you'll want to ask questions in person and learn about their background, but do some behind-the-scenes investigation too. Look up their profiles on social media before you meet in person. Learn as much as you can and make sure you feel comfortable spending time together. If you have any mutual friends, ask them a few easy questions. Arm yourself with information and try to ensure that information is accurate.

Of course, accuracy can be tough to gauge. In fact, I have several friends who dated men who were quite different from the people they claimed to be online. One in particular said he was a doctor, but it turned out he just worked in the mailroom at the hospital. For my friend, the issue here wasn't that working the mailroom was a "lesser" job but that this guy had flat-out lied about his profession. She wondered what else he could have lied about. You want someone who is honest about who they are and where they want to go in life. Someone who is "successful," not because he makes $500,000 a year, but because he is happy and fulfilled. Ensuring the people you date are honest about themselves can shield you from disappointment and emotional pain. Know who you are, be honest about who you are, and expect nothing less from a potential partner.

We will share more ways that you can protect yourself in chapter 7.

Thou Shall Set Good Boundaries

I completely lost my boundaries during the course of my marriage, and I had to spend many days, weeks, and months relearning how to create and keep them. I believe anyone who's actively dating should be a stickler for boundaries. Know which areas of your life are off-limits to suitors, know which topics you never want to discuss on a date, know which actions are deal-breakers, and know how to enforce your own core set of unwritten rules. Boundaries help define who you are. When you allow the people you date to cross or ignore them, you're sacrificing your identity and emotional security.

It can be helpful to take the time to formally write down your most important boundaries to crystallize and prioritize them. If a date insists on talking about past relationships when you've asked him not to, that might not be as grave an error as showing up at your workplace unannounced. That said, remember that once you've drawn a line and someone knowingly crosses it, you've got to take a stand. Otherwise, they may feel free to trample on your boundaries any time they want. Again, we treat people how we want to be treated.

A simple way to create extremely concrete boundaries between dating and the rest of your life is to create a separate email address or cell phone number for your dating needs. This will prevent your work and social lives from becoming entangled. It can also be a lifesaver if someone you date turns out to be unhinged or obsessive. The technology exists today to have more than one phone number that goes to your cell phone, making this easier and economical for you as well.

Consider your fiscal boundaries too. A common question that comes up in regard to money and relationships is whether it's appropriate to give a significant other a loan. As we discussed in chapter 3, I personally would not recommend it. Money boundaries are among the most important ones to enforce when you are dating, and you want to keep your money as your money. A powerful dynamic is created when you owe someone money. You feel that they have the control. That can poison a relationship and is best avoided.

Bottom line: Know what you want and need, and don't bend to please someone at your own expense, either emotionally or financially.

Thou Shall Love Thyself First

The hard truth is that you need to love yourself completely before someone else can love you. If you are a whole person, you will attract another whole person. If you are wounded or feeling lost, you need to heal yourself and know yourself and love yourself before you can authentically connect with someone else. One way to know if you truly love yourself is to spend a substantial amount of time alone. If you're completely content in your own skin, you're in a good place.

Self-love is complex, so don't beat yourself up if you need some support. Many people—particularly women—struggle to build confidence from childhood onward. Modern society doesn't cut us much slack, and the constant pressure to be beautiful, successful, and totally fulfilled can be overwhelming. I've found that working my way through my Live It List™ has helped my own self-worth grow by leaps and bounds, but you may need more direct support. You want to be happy with the authentic you. It takes time to get to know the real you and understand what makes you happy. Therapists and life coaches can be fantastic partners in building confidence and learning to love yourself. If you prefer to do this work on your own, take a peek at the Resources section at the back of this book for a few books and websites that can help you build confidence and cultivate self-love.

Thou Shall Date Through All Four Seasons

It can sometimes feel like you've known someone all your life, even if you've just met, but in reality, experts say *it takes two to four years to get to know someone.* Seeing a potential partner in a variety of settings and over the course of time is important to uncovering his true character. So be patient, and don't let outside pressures to move your relationship along influence your choices. It takes a very, very long time to truly get to know someone. If you rush into a commitment, you may not know his true character, which can lead to nasty surprises.

A matchmaker once gave me this brilliant advice: Date someone through all four seasons. There's nothing wrong with taking your time. You want to know the person you are dating on more than just the surface level, and how can you do that if you've only been dating for a short while? More and more people are waiting longer to get married, if at all. An Emory University study found that married couples who had dated for three years or more before getting hitched were 39 percent less likely to get divorced. So why rush? You feel your biological clock ticking? Well, that's not a logical reason to rush into anything. After a year has passed, you will have seen how this person responds to certain holidays and events, you'll have learned his likes and dislikes, and you'll know how he fares in good times and in rough ones. After two years, you'll know even more. (Two years is *not* that long if you truly want to get to know someone in order to spend a lifetime with them.) Take the time to get to know his friends and family, travel with him, and understand what makes him tick. Slow down and go deeper.

Thou Shall Not Send a Plant (Thou Shall <u>Really</u> Listen to What Others Want)

I went on a first date with a guy who seemed funny and nice, so I agreed to a second date. Big mistake. Once date number two began, I saw that he was trying too hard, and knew I'd misjudged our first date. He was not my type at all. I survived the second date and told him afterwards that we should just be friends. I then stopped communicating with him.

The following week, I got a phone call from a landscaping nursery stating that they had a delivery for me, and they'd been told to call this number to get an address. I gave them my address after the gal on the phone promised it would not be given out to anyone, and I asked what was being delivered. She said, "A plant from the guy you recently broke it off with." He obviously hadn't listened when I told him that I don't have a green thumb. My life is too busy, and I can't keep plants alive, which I'd specifically mentioned. What was even stranger was the note that came with the plant: "Hey … nothing says, 'Let's get to know each other better, but as a friend first' like an ugly houseplant. Right?!?!"

I'd already known that we didn't have the right chemistry. This follow-up gesture made it clear that he hadn't listened to me or processed anything I'd said about myself and my life. When you're getting to know someone, it's critical to listen to them and absorb any statements they make about themselves.

Also, don't try too hard or do something "funny" that might end up backfiring. One time, I literally received a contract from a guy after our first date. It was a funny, very tongue-in-cheek contract, but it also showed me that he was a bit crazy. Some people just seem to have too much time on their hands.

The bonus eleventh commandment is perfectly illustrated by Bachelor Brandon's story at the beginning of this chapter: Thou shall always be prepared to pay. Chapter 6 focuses on issues of payment in dating, so we'll explore this topic in depth. For now, you should never head out on a date with zero cash, maxed-out credit cards, or a frighteningly low bank balance. Dating costs money. Be prepared to pay for 100 percent of your meals and activities without expecting your date to cover all the costs. With the dating service It's Just Lunch, checks come separately since it's expected that each individual pay their own lunch tabs.

Never put yourself in a situation where you can't cover the entire cost of an evening's activities. If you're broke or drowning in debt, you might not be ready to date at all. Get right with yourself first, and your money second, and then begin your search for a life partner.

Dating Do's and Don'ts

Much of the advice in this book is drawn from stories that individuals and couples have told me as I've helped with their money matters over the years. Some is drawn from my own dating experiences. I've gone on a lot of dates with a wide variety of men. I've learned some hard lessons during my years as a single woman. I've also spoken with friends and colleagues both in person and via social media to collect stories and input. For the most part, I want what you read here to be detailed and comprehensive.

I also know that sometimes you just want a simple, practical checklist to consult before you grab your car keys and head out to happy hour with Bachelor #812.

What follows are lists of dating do's and don'ts, some from me and some from others. (Though I agree with all of them!) Many of these bullet points will seem self-explanatory, but I'm including them anyway because I've learned that it's always better to be thorough when it comes to matters of manners and etiquette.

For instance, I've met a surprisingly large number of women who believe it's perfectly appropriate to interrogate their dates, asking probing questions and digging into their personal and financial details on the first date. Some also have no issues with "testing" potential suitors to find out how smart or patient or wealthy they are. To be clear, *none of these tactics is acceptable!* During my research, I discovered that many adult women believe some of these tactics are workable. They are the driving force behind these lists.

Having said that, here are some do's and don'ts that I've collected for you from personal experiences, social media, and client stories:

Do's

Naturally, the most important "do" on any date is "be yourself." If you try to be more outgoing or energetic than you naturally are, or if you pretend to be head over heels for a guy who secretly bores you, it'll backfire fast. You can and should *be the best version of yourself* when you're out on a date. The guidelines that follow can help you do just that.

- Do be classy. (Keep profanity to a minimum, don't say unkind things about other people, steer clear of touchy subjects, don't be judgmental or dismissive, etc.)
- Do show genuine interest in the other person.
- Do be honest and kind.
- Do communicate. Don't be short, but if he does or says something that makes you upset or uncomfortable, find a way to express that. If he does or says something that makes you happy, express that too.
- Do have fun.
- Do let the man pay on a first date. (More on this in chapter 6!)
- Do focus on shared interests and adventures. You'll be far happier finding places where you overlap than places where you diverge.
- Do be polite.
- Do fall for the man he is—not who you want him to be.
- Do listen to your inner voice. Trust your gut.
- Do make eye contact.
- Do have fresh breath.
- Do be on time.
- Do give your date your undivided attention. Put your cell phone away.

- Do reciprocate by asking questions. Show mutual interest during conversations.
- Do be yourself.
- Do keep the conversation light and enjoyable.
- Do take it slow and enjoy the journey.
- Do drive yourself to the date. On a related note, do keep it short with a clear end time in case it doesn't go well.
- Do date someone who understands and supports your purpose.
- Do date someone who isn't threatened by your strengths or weaknesses.

Don'ts

Everyone has their pet peeves and turnoffs. There's no way to predict when one of your mannerisms or opinions is going to rub someone the wrong way … and when it does, that's no judgment on you. Some people just aren't meant for each other! That said, there are a few behaviors that irritate and insult nearly everyone and should be avoided on all dates.

- Don't talk about yourself the entire time. Always ask questions. Be sure to listen to the answers.
- Don't suggest dates you can't afford. Be sure not to set yourself up to date outside of your financial comfort zone in either direction.
- Don't use a coupon or Groupon on your first date.
- Don't overdo it on gifts too soon.
- Don't lie.
- Don't ask someone out on a first date via text message.
- Don't just get up and leave, even if the date is awful. Make an excuse, apologize, be polite, and *then* bail.
- Don't try to be the person you think he wants you to be. Stay true to your authentic self. You worked hard to discover and accept her.
- Don't text or be on your phone during the date.
- Don't post photos on Facebook, Instagram, or other social media on your first date.
- Don't honk in the driveway.
- Don't be rude.

- Don't date a colleague.
- Don't ask someone out on a first date with a group of your friends. Get together one-on-one somewhere nice and conducive to conversation.
- Don't look for someone to "complete you." Be complete first.
- Don't ask highly personal and detailed past relationship questions on a first date.
- Don't ask them why they are single.
- Don't sleep with them on the first date. Wait at least ninety days.
- Don't talk about your exes.
- Don't compromise on what you want in a partner.
- Don't ask how much they make the first week you meet them.
- Don't settle.

> Is there someone in your life who seems to handle their relationships remarkably well? If so, consider asking them to share *their* dating/love do's and don'ts.

Advice for Single People—from Single People

Do you know what's most insulting about being set up with someone *just because you're both single?* It assumes that all single people are the same! (It also kind of implies that even if we're not deeply desperate, we're probably not picky either.) Every single person is different, and every relationship is different.

With that in mind, I asked my single friends, clients, and colleagues to share the best advice they'd ever received about single life. The tips they shared were varied and fascinating. A few were even a bit on the bleak side like: "Stay single" and "Get a dog." Below you'll find the pearls of wisdom they shared with me and a few of my own thoughts on each piece of advice.

- *Stop focusing all your energy on looking for "the one." When you least expect it, that's when you'll find your perfect mate.*
  This can be frustrating to hear, but it's very true. Trying too hard is one of the most effective forms of self-sabotage! Do your best to

be patient and focus on building your best life instead of obsessing over hunting down your ideal mate.

- *Invest in looking your best. Make sure you love your hairstyle, makeup, and wardrobe so you'll feel confident and gorgeous on every date.*
  Absolutely! If you've already checked these boxes, don't use this advice as an excuse to get a frivolous makeover, but if you haven't updated your look in five or more years, sink some money into a personal stylist and revamp everything from hair to shoes. When you look good, you feel good. Confidence is a powerful aphrodisiac!

- *Being happy with who you are and what you've become is the best way to make yourself ready to receive love.*
  I wouldn't go so far as to say that someone struggling with self-esteem issues is totally incapable of finding a healthy relationship, but it definitely creates roadblocks. Cultivating self-love is just plain good for you, but it also primes you to accept love from another person. It can be hard work, but it's well worth the effort.

- *Count your blessings. Be grateful.*
  Have you ever met someone who actually *likes* complainers? Me neither. Don't be one! Focus on the positive and acknowledge how lucky and fortunate you are. Cultivate active gratitude. Doing this will draw other openhearted, grateful, self-aware people toward you.

- *Enjoy life by doing things you like to do. Don't limit yourself to activities that might lead to meeting someone.*
  I've brought up this concept a few times already, but I was thrilled to learn that a friend who responded to this poll was backing me up! Yes, if you're single, you should ensure that some of your regular activities are group focused instead of solitary. At the same time, you should *not* join teams or sign up for classes that don't truly interest you just to meet a mate! Enrich your life as well as the path you are on, and love will enter your lane.

- *Don't date someone just because they're wealthy. Wealth is not enough.* It can be so tempting to convince yourself that dating a wealthy man will make your life easier. You'll still have the same problems, and the money will still be his. It's perfectly fine to want to date someone who earns well, but don't make wealth your number one criterion for a mate.

- *Never lower your standards just because you're feeling desperate to find love.* The right person will come along eventually if you're patient and open.

- *Be aware that when one person wants you, you become more enticing to others. Manage this carefully and don't take advantage of it.* Most of us have experienced this phenomenon at one time or another. We've gone months without a decent date, and then one eligible bachelor emerges. Suddenly, we're fielding nonstop text messages, getting flirty looks and free drinks at the bar, and basically beating back suitors with a stick. It's human nature to find someone more alluring if you know they've piqued the interest of others. It can be very flattering to be at the center of this romantic storm. Be cautious and kind. Enjoy the attention, but don't play guys against each other. You'd never want *them* to do something like that to *you*, right?

- *When you travel with someone, you really get to know them. No need to sink thousands into a tropical vacation. Try a weekend-long road trip instead!* People act differently when they're out of their element. There is so much to learn about a person when you are able to see how they react and deal with the stresses of travel. This is true for short, affordable trips as well as luxury vacations.

- *Stop looking for what you want. Look for what you need instead.* You may *want* someone who has the Rock's physique and Brad Pitt's face, but you *need* someone who loves and accepts you just as you are. You may *want* someone who has 100 percent normal relatives and no family baggage, but you *need* someone who'll adore your kids as if they were his own. Learn the difference between a wish and a must-have.

- *Remember that looks aren't everything.*
  See above. Also remember that looks fade over time. A great personality and a deep connection just get richer and stronger as the years go by.

- *Always be yourself.*
  Well, always be *the best version* of yourself! (For help with this, refer back to the Do's and Don'ts earlier in this chapter!)

- *Stop interviewing prospects. Think of dating as getting to know people you enjoy being around.*
  I'd push back on this one just a little because I think of my speed dating process as "interviewing prospects." I know exactly what I'm looking for and can tell very quickly if someone is a real contender or not. I've also gone on many dates with people who turned out to be better for me as clients or friends than as romantic partners. The heart of this advice is to *enjoy the dating process* instead of thinking about it as a second (or third or fourth) job.

- *Don't spend big to impress your date. It will always backfire.*
  Men are more apt to do this than women. I've definitely heard some stories about gals who wanted to appear wealthier than they truly were. If your first few dates are extravagantly expensive, you're setting a precedent. Pick activities, restaurants, and bars you can afford moving forward. Doing this aligns with being your authentic self from the start.

- *Be picky.*
  Absolutely. If you're feeling lonely, or if you desperately need some help with the kids, or if your family or friends are pressuring you to settle down, it can be tough to maintain your high standards. You have just got to push through. Settling for some barely passable guy will never make you truly happy. Hold out for the real thing.

- *Keep an open mind.*
  This is absolutely essential. Writing and sticking to your Partner List can definitely help you narrow down the field, but allow some wiggle room. Sometimes it's the most unexpected person who turns out to be your dream lover. Say yes to blind dates, talk to guys in different lines of work, and go with the flow. Even if doing so doesn't lead to a perfect love match, it'll definitely supply you with some great stories!

Four Simple Rules for Modern Women

I know, I know. There are lots of rules and regulations in this chapter! I can't wrap up without sharing these four additional guidelines. They're simple, straightforward, and easy to remember. And they'll help keep you focused on and aware of your wants and needs.

Rule 1: The only thing a man should change about you is your last name.
Rule 2: Life is too short. If you want something, go get it and give it your all.
Rule 3: Let your desires and intentions be known from the beginning.
Rule 4: Don't try to find a man who'll fix your life. If you are unhappy, fix yourself first.

The best dating advice I've ever received myself? *Pay attention.* Listen to what he says—and see if it aligns with how he behaves. Take note of how he treats the people around him. Trust your gut if you feel like he's bad news. Never go out on a date and put your brain on autopilot. Stay alert, stay aware, and stay attuned.

Catfishing, Ghosting, and Gaslighting

When we talk about dating the modern age, we would be remiss to not touch a few modern-day dating issues.

Catfishing is when someone pretends to be someone they are not. You might be familiar with the TV show *Catfish* on MTV. This tends to happen online. Someone creates a fake profile, sometimes even for a member of the opposite sex, with the intention of having an online relationship with someone.

You can often spot these fake profiles by their lack of photos from different time periods or a lack of interaction with other profiles on social media. If something feels wrong, it probably is. It's important to not share too much personal information with people you don't know well or have not met.

Ghosting is when, rather than having an adult conversation about not pursuing your relationship, the other person just drops off the planet. This is where treating others how you wish to be treated comes in as well. Dating is an adult activity—communicate like an adult. If you are interacting with someone and no longer wish to see them or converse, let them know. Don't just disappear. If you are on the receiving end of being ghosted, this is not the person for you.

Gaslighting is emotionally abusive. It's when one person lies here, lies there, and makes you feel like you are crazy. Their snide comments cause self-doubt. The perpetrator is attempting to gain power by making you question your own reality. It's a common technique employed by dictators, abusers, cult leaders, and narcissists.

Gaslighting happens over time, often little by little. Again, if things don't feel right, they are not. You know yourself and what you are looking for. If you find yourself in this situation, end it!

The most important dating advice I can give you as a reader? Take all dating advice with a grain of salt! My hope is that most of what you read here will ring true and be helpful, but some of it will undoubtedly miss the mark. You know yourself better than anyone else in the world. You know the type of guy who suits you, and you know your deal-breakers. If someone offers you advice, listen carefully, process what they're saying, and decide if it applies to you. If it doesn't, thank them for their input and ignore their suggestions. If it does, try it out and pass it on. Try to remember that advice-givers nearly always have your best interests at heart—even if their actual input is *way* off the mark!

Summary

Dating can create a whirlwind of emotions, so create a few basic guidelines that will keep you grounded: Understand and love yourself before trying to partner with someone else, protect yourself and set healthy boundaries, be honest with yourself, and be patient with your relationships. Even if you feel like a dating pro, it can help to run through a list of do's and don'ts as a reality check. The bottom line is to be the absolute best version of yourself—and don't forget your manners!

> ### *Words of Wisdom*
>
> *Real love has no walls, plays no games, has clear intentions, grows in purpose, guards its unity, and always proves itself committed.*
> —Brittany Moses

5

Taking the Plunge

I went out with a guy who had been trying to charm me for quite some time. On our date, we happened to run into a mutual friend of ours. (I had no idea they knew each other.) The date suddenly went sour when that friend asked my date how his fiancée was doing. Obviously, I hadn't known he was engaged. When I found this out, the date was over immediately! The story didn't end there.

A few months later, the same guy called me again and asked me out on another date. When I asked him if he was still engaged, he said no, but I declined anyway. When I told our mutual friend about the call, he started laughing and said, "Well, technically he wasn't lying when he denied being engaged anymore because he'd gotten married in the meantime!" What the heck was that guy thinking? Did he really think I would go out with him again after that happened the first time around?

Wary Wendy

***

What do you do after you define who you are, make your Live It List™, Partner List, and decide exactly what you want in a relationship? You set the intention. You let the world know—including your friends, family, coworkers, and even your online social network—that you are ready and want to date.

Whether you are getting out into the dating world for the first time or just need a fresh perspective, allow yourself to try different activities to meet a variety of people. Don't completely disregard your list of ten (or one hundred) things you want in a partner, but don't let it dictate your choices either. I know this may seem contrary to some of my previous advice, but hear me out.

Dive Right In

When you're ready to date, just start dating. Meeting and conversing with a wide variety of people can help you determine what you want (and don't want) in a potential life partner. The list you created was part of setting your intention, and it's an incredibly important step. It's also pretty theoretical, and what sounds great in theory can be absolutely abysmal in practice. So be flexible and open, especially when you first dive into the dating pool. You should try a date with a biker, an artist, an engineer, a teacher, a politician, an attorney, a doctor, or a barista. Why not try someone who's older or younger? Meet with people from different parts of the country—or the world. Especially if you've been out of the game for a while, you might need to connect with a diverse array of personalities, professions, and backgrounds before you can clearly see which ones will and won't work for you.

Once I brought a friend to a party, and so did another friend. These two—who we will call Braden and Kiera—started talking to each other. Everyone at the party saw this instant spark when the two of them met. It was a special moment to witness. They talked, went on a few dates, and fell head over heels for each other. Even though they were in very different age brackets, they didn't let that deter them. By being open-minded, they had a marvelous time getting to know each other. It didn't work out for them in the long run for various reasons, but by accepting invitations to a party, overlooking the age gap, and keeping their hearts open, they paved the way for a fantastic dating experience. Despite not being a long-term love connection, it was an experience both learned and grew from.

We need to acknowledge as well that the more persistent you are in dating, the more likely you are to find someone to complement your life. You can't go on one or two dates and give up! It will be an investment of time, energy, and money, but dating frequently and meeting many potential partners quite literally increases your chances of meeting your match. Although it does require time and energy, making it tiring at times, frequent dating can help you learn about yourself as well as help you grow into a better person. Meeting new people forces you to focus on and practice listening, communicating, and sharing your emotions, which are all valuable skills. As we discussed in chapter 4, dating has a way of helping you understand and stick to your boundaries.

Be Bold

If you are not a naturally outgoing person, it may feel challenging to talk to people. Despite that challenge, do what you can to push back on your anxiety and be bold. We all know someone who can walk into a room and instantly light it up, making everyone want to talk to them. If you're shy or introverted, that may never be you, but you can still nudge yourself to be more daring when it comes to approaching people. You've got to learn to ask for what you want, especially now that you know what that is.

Life is too short to live with regrets. If you're sitting in a coffee shop and see someone you'd like to get to know, go talk to him. Ask him if he's tried the French roast, and if it's any good. Comment on what he is wearing or carrying. "I love your glasses. Where did you get them?" Say something to spark a conversation and find a common interest. What's the worst that can happen? He'll ignore you? Not be interested? You may walk away a little disheartened, but at least you won't kick yourself for never being courageous enough to even start a conversation.

The first commandment of dating from chapter four states, "Thou shall not appear desperate," so be sure you understand the difference between "being bold" and "chasing a guy." By all means, make the first move, strike up a conversation, and approach him. Then allow him to do the rest of the pursuing. Express your interest, then step back and let him make the next move.

> When it comes to dating, you get out what you put in. If you grumble and gripe and enter the dating pool kicking and screaming, you're unlikely to find Mr. Right. If you pour lots of positive energy and good intentions into your dating life, you'll get it back in spades.

Put Dating on Your Calendar

We've already established that dating is a numbers game. The more men you meet, the better your chances of finding the right one for you. Part of setting your intention should be literally blocking off time on your calendar for dating. Pick a couple of weeknights, a weekend evening, or an afternoon, and create time slots for dates. Then fill those slots! If you can carve out three dates per week, make your goal to *actually go on* three dates every week.

If you're a busy, successful, ambitious woman, chances are anything that isn't on your calendar won't get done. Therefore, put dating on your calendar. Make it a priority. When you make dating and yourself a priority, you let the world know you're serious about meeting your match.

If you are a single parent who has limited time in her schedule, make sure you choose your dates carefully and focus your time together on getting to know each other.

Set a Dating Budget

You'll also need to earmark money specifically for dating. If you've been out of the dating pool for a long time, you may have forgotten that meeting someone can be an expensive endeavor! Take a look at your budget and figure out approximately how much to put aside for dating costs. These might include:

- fees for online dating sites, or a professional matchmaker
- cab/car fare
- meals and beverages
- date activities (movies, concerts, etc.)
- hair, makeup, or any additional grooming you wouldn't otherwise be doing
- personal trainer or gym membership fees to keep yourself in great shape (if you are looking for a fit partner, you should be a fit partner)

- gifts (more of a concern deeper into relationships, but still comes up)
- travel expenses

Naturally, you won't be expected to pay for both yourself and your date every time you go out (more on this in chapter 6). You should be prepared to pay for your own half of everything, even if you aren't asked to. If you're seriously and actively dating, consider setting aside 3–5 percent of your income to cover the various costs. If that sounds like a lot, talk to a few single men. They believe they invest more in finding someone to date than their female counterparts do!

Now, 3–5 percent is a pretty sizable chunk, so bear in mind that you should only earmark it for dating costs if you're very wise with your income and how you spend it. If you make $70K and spend 5 percent of your income on a dating budget, that is $3,500 that could have gone into your 401(k), IRA, savings, or investment account, or to pay down your mortgage faster. If you make $300K, you're sinking $15K per year into dating, which is probably more than you'll need. In my opinion as long as you max out your retirement plans and are on track financially, you can go for the full 5 percent. It's up to you to keep a clear head and prioritize. When it comes to dating, you are going to get out of it what you put into it. The goal is to spend on experiences and activities you'd pursue and enjoy on your own—even if you weren't dating. If you aren't enjoying movies and dinners with men you pay one hundred dollars a month to meet on Match.com, I'd rather see you spend one hundred dollars a month on something you'd truly enjoy.

How to Talk about Dating

Part of being intentional about dating is making it very clear to just about everyone in your network that you're interested and available. That means talking about dating and what you are looking for in a partner, potentially more openly and frequently than you're used to. Doing this may make you uncomfortable at first, but it means that everyone you share with will be thinking of you when they meet other single people, who might fit your partner list. Their antennae will be buzzing, and when they hear that a fantastic guy friend with the qualities you are looking for is seeking a partner, you'll be top of mind. If your network of friends knows you are single and what you are looking for, they become a resource you can utilize in your journey to finding an ideal partner.

That said, there are smart, strategic ways to discuss your dating life, and there are ill-advised, destructive ways to do it. Here are a few do's and don'ts:

- Do talk about how much fun you have on dates. Keep a positive spin as much as possible.
- Don't complain about how hard dating is or how you're not meeting anyone worthwhile. Doing this doesn't make you enticing to anyone.
- Do highlight the cool activities you try with the men you're meeting. This shows how interesting, adventurous, and open-minded you are!
- Don't mention dates by name or post photos of you together unless you've both agreed that you're comfortable with that level of exposure. (Tagging or calling out dates by name may also broadcast that you're more "together" than you really are, discouraging other dating opportunities.)
- Do tell close friends and family that you're in the market. Be sure to describe what you're looking for in a partner.
- Don't get as specific when talking with colleagues and acquaintances as you would with friends and family.
- Do smile.
- Don't dwell on negative subjects.
- Do be open to giving compliments.
- Don't get caught up in comparing dates or suitors. Focus on what's good about each experience or person instead of "keeping score."
- Do ask for restaurant and activity suggestions from friends, family, and colleagues.
- Don't ask for dating advice from acquaintances or coworkers.
- Do ask for dating advice from the truly successful and happy couples you know.
- Do talk about what you've learned about yourself by meeting interesting new people.

Your romantic life is private, but unless you're willing to talk about your intentions, you may inadvertently shut down potential avenues for meeting people. When you're searching for a new job, you tell your contacts to keep their eyes peeled on your behalf, right? If you're searching for a new partner, doesn't it make sense to do the same? By talking about dating, you tell the world you're here, you're ready, and you're open. Be sure you talk about it strategically and positively.

Understanding the Stages of Dating

When you're entering or reentering the world of dating, it's helpful to know what to expect. Dating follows some predictable stages, and when you're aware of them and understand what they entail, you can be savvy about how you comport yourself. While I'd encourage you to dive right in and meet a variety of men, you need to be prepared for how your budding relationships will play out. Otherwise, you may misinterpret emotional signals or get invested too soon.

Here's how most new romantic relationships break down:

Stage 1

This is the three-to-six-month time period of dating when you're feeling giddy, glowing, and happy. Your friends know something is different. You walk with a lighter step because you are falling in love. Many refer to this as "the honeymoon stage." It feels great, but it can also be a little misleading. Both people are on their absolute best behavior, and hopes are high. Everyone is following the Ten Commandments of Dating, and excitement is in the air. (Everything in the first three months is really just getting-to-know-each-other time in most cases. That time isn't a true stage, especially if you are dating multiple people.)

Stage 2

Most people move past the honeymoon stage about six months into dating. Around this time, you get more comfortable with each other. Fears and weaknesses start to show through, but lasting trust is also being built. This is a key time when a few deal-breakers may begin to emerge. You begin to discover each other's true colors.

Stage 3

After one year of dating, you've known someone through every season. You have met his family and friends and vice versa. You've talked about credit reports, financial priorities, and budgets. By this time, you'll have an inkling about whether or not this is "the one," the person with whom you'd consider spending the rest of your life.

Honestly speaking, I really believe it takes at least three years to get to know someone thoroughly and completely. It seems to me that if people slowed down a little and spent real time with their potential partners before marrying them, the divorce rate wouldn't be quite so high! For most of year one—even once you move beyond the honeymoon phase—you're still pretty blissed out and starry-eyed about each other. Year two is when personality quirks emerge as you gain a deeper familiarity with each other. By year three, you will know if your quirks and true selves are compatible for the rest of your life.

We've already touched on the importance of taking it slow and not rushing your relationships. In my opinion, the fact that these three stages exist further reinforces that idea. Until you've spent a full year dating someone—letting your lives and friends and families intertwine—you won't have any idea what it would be like to spend your lives together. When you fall hard for someone in those first few months, you can feel so sure that they're your twin flame, but you won't know for certain until you've moved beyond the honeymoon stage, seen some of their flaws (and let them see yours), and been through some tough times together.

If you're getting back into dating after a long lapse, you may have forgotten that these stages even exist. They create a predictable rhythm that most budding romances follow. Keep them in mind as you start meeting and becoming involved with new people. You'll be better prepared for the natural ups and downs of new romance.

One thing I want you to keep in mind while reading this book is that there is nothing at all wrong with choosing to remain single. Society and social contacts pressure us to believe that being single somehow makes you inadequate. That is a myth! Being single can be a choice—not just a circumstance.

Throughout this book and the self-exploration you will engage in, don't be surprised if you want to date yourself for a while. Self-care, self-reflection, and investing in yourself is a surefire win for you.

The same goes for marriage and children. Having a uterus does not somehow make you contractually obligated to procreate. There was a time where a woman's only option for a life was marriage. In the early 1970s, a single female couldn't have a credit card unless she was married, and her husband added her on to his account.

This is not the world we live in today, despite the societal pressures that still exist for women to settle down, marry, and have children. Women today have a choice, and we have more opportunities than the women who came before us did.

Marriage and children are beautiful choices, but they need to be your choice and not anyone else's. This is why we start out discovering ourselves and building a foundation around our own needs and wants, separating the needs or wants of others that may have been put upon us.

Summary

Digging into dating can feel overwhelming, but the key is to trust the process. Be open and date a variety of people. Be bold and ask for what you want. Make dating a priority, on your calendar, in your bank account, and in your communications. Jump in with both feet—and enjoy the ride!

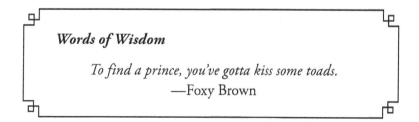

Words of Wisdom

To find a prince, you've gotta kiss some toads.
—Foxy Brown

6

To Pay or Not to Pay

We went out to dinner for our first date. When it came time to pay the sixty-dollar tab, he proceeded to take out a coupon that he had purchased for twenty dollars, which was good for forty dollars' worth of food. He then proceeded to tell me that he expected me to pay the remainder of the bill and the tip since he was paying for "forty dollars" of the dinner. Obviously, there was not a second date. Sure, it's great that he's financially focused and conservative with his money, but this behavior on a first date is just plain inappropriate. Not to mention rude.

Brooke the Bridesmaid

***

Dating today is very different than it was ten, twenty, or thirty years ago. Social norms and expectations have changed, people have changed, and the dating landscape has shifted radically. Since it continues to shift and change all the time, it can be difficult to know what to expect.

This is especially true when it comes to money. Once upon a time, when our grandparents were courting each other, there were cut-and-dried gender roles that made the question of "Who should pay the bill at the end of the evening?" a nonissue. As women began to take on different roles and responsibilities, as well as work to gain more equality across many areas of life, things got murky. Now with gender fluidity and same-sex couples, figuring out finances based on gender can feel positively passé!

Let's say you know exactly what you want. You have your Partner

List, so you go online seeking the person you think will meet your needs. You find a likely candidate and agree to meet for coffee. Since you get to the café early, you go ahead and buy your own drink. He arrives later and buys his own too. The two of you hit it off and eagerly arrange for a second date later that week. You meet at a restaurant you love, a casual spot that is moderately priced. You have an appetizer, some drinks, and a lovely dinner. So far, pure bliss! Then the server comes with the check. Now what do you do?

He works, and you work. You think you make approximately the same amount of money. You want to assert your independence, but you also don't want to insult him. So, do you offer to buy the whole dinner? Offer to pay half? Not offer at all?

Unfortunately, there's no clear-cut correct answer, regardless of circumstances. In this chapter, we'll walk through a few scenarios and explore the factors you'll want to consider as you decide how to handle paying for your dates.

The Advantages of Offering

A longtime client once told me that when the date has ended and the bill comes to the table, you can tell a lot about the character and intentions of the other person by how he responds when you ask if you can contribute to the tab. Simply by offering, you can eliminate any feelings of guilt or worries about freeloading. Plus, by carefully observing his reaction, you can gather information about what he's thinking.

Now, you may be looking to meet a man who would say, "Oh, no need," when you ask to go dutch on a first date. You may want a traditional male, someone who feels proud and happy when he can provide for the people in his life. (I'll freely admit this is my preference. I like it best when my date discreetly hands his credit card to the server before the check even arrives. This approach eliminates any awkward moments and shows he can take charge.) Even if this is the case, I would urge you to *still offer to chip in*, even if you hope he'll decline. Remember to always have the money available in the event that he does accept your offer.

Or perhaps you're coming at payment from a very different angle. You might not want to feel beholden to anyone and truly prefer to pay for your own meal. You've worked hard, you're proudly independent, and you're not interested in being taken care of. You want someone who will treat you as an equal partner, across the board. One of the hardest things for independent-minded women is to allow a man to help. Men want to feel needed. It gives them confidence and helps them feel secure. For some women, watching a man insist on paying at the end of the date actually raises red flags! It just depends how you're wired and what you like.

Survey Says

I conducted a poll on my personal Facebook page to gauge opinions on dating and money. I wanted to learn what people of all genders believed to be the acceptable and appropriate way to handle payment responsibilities on a date. About fifty of my friends, colleagues, and clients responded. Here's a summary of my findings:

- 80 percent of respondents said they felt the man should pay the whole tab on the first date. Many stated that a true gentleman would offer to pay for everything, and if his date offered to contribute, he wouldn't accept. One man wrote, "I believe in courtship, remember what that is? A guy pays on the first date. Not because the woman can't pay or to make her feel inferior. The intention is the exact opposite: it's to praise her and show appreciation for her. This idea seems to have faded for whatever reason, but it's a simple concept called chivalry!"

- 13 percent said that whoever initiated the date should pay the whole tab. One woman noted, "If I ask someone out, then I anticipate I will be the one to pay." Another said that she handles this by excusing herself toward the end of the meal to go to the restroom, then flags down the server on her way to hand over her credit card. That way, the tab is fully paid, and there's no awkward moment when the bill arrives.

- 7 percent said that each person should pay for their own meal or split the bill. This keeps things simple. One woman wrote "On the first date, I usually go 50/50, unless the guy asked me out and insists on paying for everything. If I don't hit it off with the guy,

I *always* pay for my own, so I don't give him the impression that I want another date."

These results surprised me. I honestly expected more people to want to pay their own way or have mixed feelings. The ones who went against the grain were adamant about their reasons, but the vast majority went the traditional route. Most respondents felt the man should pay regardless of circumstances—at least on the first date.

In *The End of Men*, Hanna Rosin states that more and more women are taking the initiative and asking out men. If men are too intimidated to ask a woman out and she makes the first move, should she expect to pay? According to those polled, the answer is generally no.

This interesting insight was also shared with me by a male colleague:

> Online dating options such as Tinder, Match, etc. play a role in introducing you to other single people, people you otherwise wouldn't have met in real life. Sounds great, right? But while there may be a physical attraction based on dating profile photos, and even a perceived chemistry based on text or phone conversations that follow after you have a "match," I'm of the mind-set that you can't really get to know someone until you spend time with them face-to-face. That usually means getting together for drinks and a few appetizers. As a guy, I feel obligated to pay, since it's what society says is the appropriate thing to do. The first date could cost about $40–50. Overall, not too bad, but how much can you really surmise about a woman based on a first date? Assuming that date number one goes well enough for there to be a second date, maybe that second date comes in the form of going to a baseball game or comedy club or dinner at a decent restaurant. That second date could cost more than $100. Again, not a huge amount but even after date number two, I'm still trying to feel the person out. Go out on a couple other dates, and the next thing I know I've spent $300–400 on someone who ultimately isn't going to become my

girlfriend. Then I have to start the process all over again with someone new and hope for a different outcome! Sure, there are less expensive ways to get to know someone than dinner or ballgames ... hiking or taking a long walk, for instance, but during the winter [in the Midwest], those options won't work. In the end, I've chosen to limit the amount of dates I go on because of the cost.

Understanding Your Payment Priorities

April Davis, founder of LUMA Luxury Matchmaking, states that both parties should come up with a "fair" payment agreement in advance. You pay for "ABC," and I will cover "XYZ," all hammered out before the actual dates take place. Of course, fair is subjective depending on the two people. If one person is a public school teacher and the other is a high-powered investment banker, the investment banker can't expect the teacher to pay for half of everything. Regardless of income breakdown, Davis believes that the man should generally pay for two-thirds of restaurant meals. She also points out that, if the woman makes less money, she could occasionally offer to cook dinner for her date to help make it "fair." I'd add that couples could consider splitting their dating expenses based on each person's percentage of total income. If he makes $40K and you make $60K, he'll pay for 40 percent and you'll pay for 60 percent.

All of these ideas are helpful once you are in a serious relationship, but what about when you are just beginning to date?

The answer to who should pay really depends on what you want. Is it more important to you that your partner be generous and eager to make you feel pampered? Or do you want clear-cut boundaries and full acknowledgement of your independence? Or perhaps something in between? It's important for you to understand your wants and acknowledge the root sources of those wants.

In my case, I want to date a true gentleman. This means I want someone who will pay on the first date. That doesn't mean that I won't offer, or that I haven't paid for the whole tab myself on many dates. I will do it, but my interest in a potential partner quickly dissipates if he always expects me to cover both of our costs. If a man takes advantage of the fact that I'm willing to pay all the time, it leaves a bad taste in my mouth. That said, I'm happy to pay for the date activity in advance and let my date cover dinner. For example, if the date was dinner and go-kart racing, I would prepay for the racing, and then at the restaurant, the guy would pay in public. This way, he doesn't feel emasculated, and I feel good about contributing.

Have you ever gone on a series of dates that *didn't* make you worry about money matters at all? Who paid? When? Was it easy and seamless because he paid for everything without even asking—or did you discuss money matters before meeting in person? What worked and why? How can you recreate those circumstances moving forward?

If money is always a concern when you begin to date someone new, think about how to mitigate that. Would you feel better if you talked about your expectations before the first date and communicated your needs ahead of time? Or would you rather set some internal rules for yourself but leave enough wiggle room to make decisions on the fly? Give some thought to what will make you feel the most secure and comfortable and then stick to that on future dates.

Dealing with Social Anxiety Around Money

Today, some women make more money than men, a situation that was virtually unheard of just a few decades ago. Other women are completely financially independent and simply *want* to pay for things on their own. Of course, a few women who've settled down end up partnering with stay-at-home dads who raise the kids while they work.

Some women who find themselves in these gender role-reversal positions have great relationships with their partners, while others struggle. It completely depends on how well each couple communicates and the work they've put into finding systems that work for them both.

I know a woman who started seeing a man who met her typical dating criteria. She fell hard for him fast. It was a great romance, plus they seemed totally compatible ... except when it came to money. She made a significant amount more than he did, and whenever she thought about their long-term prospects, she worried. If she wanted the two of them to go to Italy for two weeks, would she have to pay for the entire trip herself? Would she feel comfortable covering all costs for the things she wanted to do since he couldn't to afford to meet her halfway? Luckily, he made the decision easy for her. He failed to step up and show his support in other areas. She soon realized it would never be a full and healthy partnership. Eventually, they broke it off.

To be clear, their relationship didn't end simply because of a potential trip to Italy. It ended because he didn't offer her the support she needed financially or emotionally. If he had supported her emotionally in her business and her life, it might have worked despite their income disparity. (If he'd had a different disposition, the fact that she outearned him might've made him feel emasculated. Many men's confidence takes a dip when they find out a woman they're dating makes more money.)

The best way to deal with money-based anxiety is to address it head-on. With anything—but especially with money—it all comes down to communication. Before you get too deep into a relationship, you need to make sure you share the same values when it comes to money matters. If you don't, you need to find ways to get on the same page.

This is especially important because as women, we are expected to juggle work and home life without ever missing a beat. Working women, stay-at-home moms, and single mothers struggle with the issue of balance and how to do it all. As Sheryl Sandberg states in *Lean In,* women work more hours and care for the kids more than their male counterparts. We're still a long way away from real gender equity in the office and at home, which makes it even more crucial to partner with men who share your money mind-set. Otherwise, you may end up feeling overworked and taken for granted.

Plan Ahead, Be Clear

So, what do you do if you make more money than someone you'd like to date? Well, if you make it an issue, it will be an issue. If money is something that is extremely important to you, it may grow into a bigger issue than you'd anticipate. If it will put your mind at ease to have an up-front conversation about money, then do that. If you want to wait until you're a few dates in to see how things play out, that's fine too. The important thing is to trust your gut and follow your instincts. Be sure to check in with yourself mentally and emotionally as the relationship progresses to see if you need to make any adjustments or have any conversations to help course correct.

If you decide that dating someone who outearns you is essential, trust that instinct. It certainly eliminates the potential for certain types of social awkwardness. In fact, some women choose to date older men because they're generally wealthier, more established in their careers, and more emotionally mature. Sticking with successful older men also lessens the chance that a woman will end up surpassing her partner on the ladder to the top.

Whatever you decide, think through your reasoning and make choices that suit your needs and lifestyle. Don't set yourself up for failure. If you ask someone out on a date and offer to pay for the whole thing but then realize you cannot afford it, be honest with yourself and with him. Either cancel the date or ask if you could split the costs instead. This may sting a little in the moment, but it sets an important precedent. You don't want to live beyond your means, and you certainly don't want to present a false impression of yourself to someone new. That's a recipe for disaster.

It's important to be authentic from the start. If you don't have a lot of money, don't flaunt it like you do. If you are of modest means and ask someone out on a date, which you expect to pay for, take him to a place you know you can afford. Don't put yourself into debt trying to impress him (or trick him into believing you're something you're not). Dating beyond your means may get you emotionally invested in a relationship that you can't afford. When he inevitably finds out the truth about your finances, he may feel betrayed. You don't want to end up in a relationship that's unsustainable.

> Authenticity is essential. Consider crafting an elevator speech that describes who you are as a person: three or four sentences that summarize your personality, talents, ambitions, and dreams. Having this knowledge on hand will help you remain true to yourself as you meet new people.

What We Want, What We Expect

Many men falsely believe that *all* women expect to be wined, dined, and impressed. Of course, many of us do, but there are exceptions. Plenty of women work hard to have their own money and financial resources, who would never expect a man they're dating to shell out for everything himself. There are also plenty of *men* who would prefer to find a partner who's willing to meet them halfway. I believe both men and women want to be appreciated, and that appreciation can manifest in ways other than picking up the tab after a date.

In fact, most people have specific ways in which they show affection and others in which they like to receive affection and appreciation. I highly recommend *The Five Love Languages* by Gary Chapman, which delves into these specific modes of emotional expression, how to identify them in yourself and your partner, and how to navigate any differences. His insights helped me understand what I need and seek in my relationships. His advice clued me into what others might require and expect of me in return.

I contributed to a story for the TV program *The List* in which producers conducted on-the-street interviews across America to ask men and women about money. The goal was to find out who saves and who spends more money. Most men said they wanted to spend money now, and they emphasized spending it on wining and dining their dates. My first question was: Where are these men, and why aren't more of them in *my* life? My second question was: Can they really afford to do that? It was clear that some of them offered this answer to the producers because it's what they thought was expected of them. That made me wonder how many of them responded more strongly to other love languages but were too shy to say so.

To be successful at dating, both parties must be honest and authentic. For your part, that means presenting yourself as you are now instead of projecting who you wish to be. If you have audacious goals, dreams, and desires, I'm not saying to ignore them. Share your vision openly, but be up-front about who you actually are today. Maintaining a personal baseline of honesty will help you find a partner who can help you achieve those audacious goals, dreams, and desires by accepting you now and supporting you into your shared future.

Summary

When it comes to paying for a date, always offer (and be prepared) to pay for your half—even if you'd prefer that he pick up the bill. If you make more money than your date or worry incessantly about issues of financial equity, don't be afraid to open a conversation and set some ground rules. It's better to be up-front about your expectations than to sabotage a relationship before it even gets started! Understand and express your financial priorities.

Words of Wisdom

I don't want a halfway kind of life. I live full. I work hard. And I love passionately. I am not built for less than everything; so, if you can't give me your all, then give me nothing.
—Nicole Lyons

7

Protecting Yourself and Your Money

I became interested in a man—let's call him Juan, since I never knew who he really was. He had a gorgeous profile picture, said he was a sports agent, and lived a couple of states away from me. He started an online conversation that I thought was about business, but it soon took a romantic turn. After messaging back and forth and doing quite a bit of e-flirting, he told me he wanted to meet. Shortly after that, he told me he'd booked a flight. I got excited! Here I was, feeling raw, with not an ounce of confidence, and someone was hopping on a plane to see me! Well, a few days before he was supposed to arrive, all of a sudden, he said he couldn't make it. He sent me a picture of a boy who he claimed was his son and told me a story about how he was desperately sick in the hospital. Not long after that, he asked me for money, at which point I knew it was a scam. Later, I learned there were many other women who fell for this ploy and actually sent this guy money!

Mamacita Marissa

***

How do you really get to know a person you're dating? As you've already learned, one way is to date him through all four seasons. Another is to spend time getting to know his friends and family. If you're a cautious person by nature, or if a guy you're interested in seems sketchy, you could also consider doing some research on your own using Google and social media. We live in an age of identity theft, fake online profiles, and catfishing schemes, so making sure a guy is who he claims to be is a legitimate concern.

During the stretch of time between the end of my marriage and the start of my dating life, I broke down and read the entire *50 Shades of Grey* series. After reading these books, I found my own Mr. Grey, at least in the emotional sense. He was the first person to take a real interest in helping me find myself and learn what life was all about. In a way, he became my relationship mentor for a short period of time. He taught me that I needed to be a whole person before I could partner with someone else.

And perhaps more importantly, he taught me that I needed to protect what I'd worked so hard to achieve. Now I want to pass along that nugget of wisdom to you: You want to be emotionally open and willing to connect with the people you date, but you also need to keep your head and watch your back, both emotionally and financially. I've watched too many clients get married too quickly—in both first and second marriages—and not protect themselves.

Basic Backup Plans

You'd never enter a business deal without first crafting an exit strategy, right? So why would you agree to meet a total stranger without first assessing how you can gracefully extract yourself, should you need to make a quick exit? Always plan ahead and know how to bail safely, in case you need to.

When you meet someone for the first time, meet at a neutral location (as opposed to meeting at your place or his) and keep it light and public. Think a quick coffee, lunch, or happy hour. And even if your first meeting feels safe and easy, have a backup plan in place. You may just *want* to cut the date short, or you may find you *need* a hasty retreat. It's not that uncommon to connect with someone online, then meet them in person and discover their profile is chock-full of lies. If that happens, don't waste your time—no matter how handsome or charming the guy may seem. You need to protect yourself from the crazy people out there, and anyone who lies on a profile page is undoubtedly hiding more than just a few personal details. A person who lies about the basic things about themselves is often hiding something more.

Always have an exit strategy in case things don't go well or in case they end up going *too* well. What if the person you're with starts getting physical before you're ready? What if you find yourself in an unsafe situation? Do you know what you'd do? Here are a few ways to safely get out of a date that's turned sour:

- Ask a friend or family member to text or call you forty minutes into the date. If things are going well, you can just say a few quick words and hang up. If you need to bail, that call or text can become a "personal emergency" that allows you to leave early. This takes some planning, but it is incredibly effective.

- Enlist the help of a staff member. Excuse yourself to the restroom, then let your server, barista, or bartender know you're feeling unsafe and need help. Depending on the situation, they can just keep an eye out for you, or fabricate a phone call through the cafe/restaurant landline so you can take the "personal emergency" escape route.

- Fake a migraine. Say you've got a massive headache coming on and need to head home to get it under control. It doesn't matter if this seems implausible—it gives you an automatic out.

A couple of other protective best practices include:

- Download the "Find My Friend" app. This allows you to keep track of friends and family who have shared their locations. They will appear on a map, so you can quickly see where they are and what they're up to. Ask your mom/friend/lifeline to download the app too and check in as soon as you arrive for your date. That way, someone always knows where you are and can help if something goes wrong.

- Text the details. Before you go out on a date, send a text to a trusted friend that includes where you are going, what you are wearing, your date's name, the agenda, etc.

- Take a basic self-defense class. This is just a good idea for any woman in today's world. Most towns and cities offer classes at martial arts studios or through community education programming. It's so easy to freeze up when things get physically uncomfortable, but with a little training, you can know exactly how to react if someone pushes things too far.

Of course, having a backup plan isn't always about personal safety. Sometimes it's more about personal preference. Once I went on a date with a guy who spent the whole time talking about himself. I was bored stiff and wanted out. When I took out my credit card to pay for my own drink, he said, "You don't need to pay for my drink." He was so entranced by the sound of his own voice that he'd never even noticed I'd ordered wine for myself. (I needed it to help me get through his deeply boring monologue.) When I finally got a word in edgewise, I used it to politely excuse myself from the date.

After a slew of disappointing and annoying first dates, I learned my lesson. I made sure that the first meeting was something short and casual, a date that wouldn't waste my time or money. Most of the time, I would just ask for a glass of water and chat with the guy for half an hour. I also learned to schedule meetings close on the heels of my first dates, providing me with an easy (and legitimate) way out. I found out the hard way that I needed to trust my first impressions, and that if someone seemed like a bad fit within the first thirty minutes, he probably was. My string of crummy first dates also reminded that time really is money. I have so few hours to spare each day—and no desire to waste them on a mismatch.

I'm sure you feel the same way, and I would urge you to guard your time. Next, we'll dive into the nitty-gritty details of guarding your money.

Don't Loan Him Money

In case you skipped or skimmed chapter 3, here's one of the most important takeaways: Asking to borrow money is a *huge* red flag. This may sound so simple and self-evident, but I have heard so many stories of smart, savvy women and men getting scammed out of cash while dating, and those stories make my blood run cold. It's important to let yourself be somewhat vulnerable when you're getting to know someone new, since you need to let them get to know you, good, bad, and ugly. If you allow yourself to be open to someone who literally steals your money, it can be hard to trust anyone ever again.

When someone you're dating asks for money, you should immediately be on your guard. If you've never met him in person, forget it. There's no way giving or lending him money is a smart move. If he asks you for money on the first, second, or third date, is he truly someone you want to date? My take is no! Absolutely not! Run away as fast as you can! This includes if he forgot his wallet, doesn't have the app to purchase the movie tickets, or didn't make it to the ATM.

A relationship is a give-and-take, but when it comes to handing out cash, you need to put yourself first and protect yourself as well as your financial health.

Think Carefully About Moving to Be Near Him

On the surface, this might not seem like an issue related to protecting yourself and your money, but it is. If you make a strong emotional connection with a man who lives in a different state (or country), should you move to be with him? Doing so might mean selling your house, quitting your job to find a new one, leaving behind your family and friends, finding new schools for the kids, covering the expenses of packing up a household, and moving everything to a new location.

Doing so could also mean a grand new adventure with someone you love madly. It might mean finding better job prospects in a new town or moving to a more affordable area where you can spring for a bigger or better condo. It might mean massive but positive changes.

Whatever you do, don't rush into this decision. If you've only ever met online, do not even *consider* uprooting yourself. Unless you've dated someone for at least two years, moving to be together and uprooting your life is out of the question.

Beyond that, be open-minded. If the guy you've fallen for lives in a town or location that you just plain loathe—a city you can't stand or a rural area where you'll be bored stiff—negotiate. See if he'd consider moving to be near you instead. If he lives somewhere that appeals to you, consider your options. If you have kids or are still in the building phases of your career, consider those factors very carefully. Your rebuilding process will be costly and challenging, and you need to weigh the pros and cons. If you're in your early twenties and haven't put down roots, or are retired and ready for a change, why not move?

Bigger Financial Hypotheticals

Naturally, when it comes to your assets, you want to have a backup plan as well. This holds true regardless of whether or not you're currently dating, but it becomes especially important when you're in the process of looking for a partner. Dating itself has money-related pitfalls, as we explored in chapter 6, but entering a serious relationship takes your financial considerations to a whole new level. You *must* have your own affairs in order before you consider merging households with another person. Also, you must make sure that your partner is going to help you, not hinder you, as you strive to meet your financial goals. You're looking for a cocaptain and not cargo.

Smart financial planning is a continuous process, and the main focus should be examining the what-if's of your life. Some of them include:

- What if I lose my job?
- What if my ex-spouse dies?
- What if I die?
- What if I get married?
- What if I get pregnant?
- What if my parents die?
- What if I get in a car accident?
- What if my child is hurt?
- What if I have a medical emergency?
- What if I become disabled?
- What if my house burns down?
- What if I lose my business?

These are just examples, and depending on your life circumstances, there may be other what-if's to add or a completely different set. You can generate your own list by thinking about where your money comes from and where it goes.

Once you've made your what-if list, do your best to address each question honestly and thoroughly. If you have a medical emergency, how will you handle it? Who will step in to take care of the kids? How much will your insurance cover? Do you have enough in your savings account to cover any deductibles? What will happen at work? It can be taxing and overwhelming to think about all of these frightening hypothetical situations, but it is essential that you do so. Financial planning is all about being prepared. If you walk through these questions and create feasible and actionable plans, you will be able to cope with any financial eventuality.

You'll have a much easier time relaxing and enjoying your life, knowing you've got your bases covered.

> When you worry about money, what's the one thing that concerns you the most? What can you do to address it? If you're having trouble facing it head-on, who or what could help you tackle it?

The Importance of Estate Planning

One of the most difficult what-if's to address is "What if I die?" No one likes to talk about this topic, but avoiding it can lead to disaster, especially for those you leave behind. Estate-planning basics address the distribution of your possessions, but more importantly, they outline how you'll take care of your loved ones. As a single person, this may seem like a low priority, but even young or unmarried folks need to consider their estates. These considerations become more pressing once you've found a partner, but the sooner you start the planning process, the better off you'll be. If you are single and have someone who is financially dependent upon you, estate planning is even more vital.

You may think you don't have an estate plan, but you do—even if you've never prepared one yourself! When you lack a formal plan, federal and state rules will kick in to determine who gets what and how much is dispersed should you pass away. It also determines how you will be treated if you should become very ill. If you are not prepared with basic estate-planning knowledge, that lack of preparation can cost you a lot of money and cause unnecessary headaches.

Putting your estate in order can be complex, depending on how many assets you have, where they are held, your family structure, state laws, and more. At a minimum, you'll want to meet with an estate-planning attorney to discuss your situation and cover a few basics. Make sure you choose someone who specializes in estate planning. Don't waste your time with an attorney who does family, criminal, or estate law and a little bit of estate planning on the side. Go with an expert who is well versed in the laws of your state of residence.

Don't attempt to cook something up on your own! Most of the estate planning attorneys I know say they'd rather a client did nothing than try to create a will or trust herself, fabricate something using online tools not accurate for their state, or partner with someone who is not an expert.

Before you dive into estate planning, consider tackling some essentials like creating a plan to protect your liquid money and paying off your credit cards. (If you have credit card debt, you are living beyond your means or a medical or health issue, divorce, death, or emergency has happened.) When you don't need money is when you should ask for it. This might mean getting a home equity line of credit on your home in case of emergencies. It might mean saving toward the goal of having six to twelve months of income set aside in liquid money.

No matter how small or large your estate is, here are the basic elements of estate planning that should be addressed.

Will or Trust

Your will shows your wishes for the disposition of your assets. It outlines how property held in your name should be distributed, names an executor to be in charge of carrying out your wishes, and provides for payments of costs incurred in settling your estate. If you have any children under the age of eighteen, your will or trust will also designate guardians and name trustees to protect their inheritance. This is where things may get difficult. How do you pick who will take care of your kids if or when you pass away? This is upsetting to think about, but consider what might happen if you *don't* give it due thought.

Durable Power of Attorney

Your durable power of attorney is a document that gives someone else permission to manage your affairs should you become disabled or incapacitated. Let's say you end up in a coma; unless you've established durable power of attorney ahead of time, your spouse (or your mom or dad or kids) cannot write out a check from your checking account, move money from your savings, change something in your 401(k), or otherwise handle your finances without your authorization. With it, as soon as you become incapacitated, your designated person is able to manage your affairs. You can set any parameters you want and restrict this power to specific assets or accounts if you wish. Don't wait! You won't be able to establish a durable power of attorney once you're incapacitated.

Health Care Directive

A health care directive is a crucial and basic estate-planning tool that designates someone to make health care decisions on your behalf if you're unable to make them yourself. Talk to the person you have in mind before appointing them to ensure they understand and are comfortable with your wishes. Also make sure that they're strong enough to carry out those wishes despite family member objections if you anticipate your wishes being contentious.

Life Insurance

When was the last time you reviewed your life insurance coverage? Have there been any changes in your life since you first purchased your policy, such as a new house? You want to make sure that you are keeping up-to-date and reviewing your terms periodically. Do you have more dependents than when you purchased your insurance? Have your life circumstances changed in other ways? With debt, liabilities, or more, you may need to add to or adjust your coverage. Periodic check-ins help ensure you've got the appropriate amount of coverage and that your beneficiaries are current. Life insurance isn't just for married people! You can take out a policy to protect yourself, your partner, or your estate at any time.

Disability Insurance

This often-overlooked type of insurance provides coverage in the event of an occupational mishap resulting in disability and provides compensation for you as an injured worker. It is not just an injury at work but could be from any type of accident. Many of us never ponder how we would continue to provide for our families if we become permanently disabled, but it's a crucial consideration. You may have an employer-sponsored disability plan, but if you don't, you'll need to purchase an individual plan. It can be frustrating to sink so much money into various types of insurance, but the alternative is grim. You want to be adequately prepared for the future in case you are unable to work and still need to provide an income for your family.

Property Insurance

Did you know that documenting your belongings can save you a world of hassle if you have to file an insurance claim? The Insurance Information Institute runs a website called www.KnowYourStuff.org where you can download free home inventory software. This will help you create a pictorial archive of all the stuff you own, including big items like your house, car, and computer, but also smaller ones like mobile phones, artwork, and clothing. Inventorying your possessions is the first step toward making sure you have sufficient insurance to cover your belongings in the event of a loss. It will also prove helpful in getting insurance claims settled faster and substantiating losses for your income tax returns.

Any estate-planning attorney worth his or her salt will address all of these topics with you, but bring the list along just in case. When it comes to your long-term financial security, you want to make absolutely sure the basics are covered.

When Should You Have the Money Talk?

Now that we've covered the essentials of protecting yourself and your assets in general, let's switch back to the world of dating. Naturally, you won't want to chat about savings goals and estate planning on a first date, but you've got to broach the subject at some point. How and when do you do that?

To fully protect yourself and your finances, you need to know the following things about anyone you choose to date seriously and exclusively:

- personal and work background
- current credit score
- financial history, including any bankruptcies
- financial stability (how much in savings, debt load, etc.)
- risky investments

The following questions should also be addressed:

- Is he on track to retire?
- How will he meet his future cash-flow needs?
- Is he a spender or a saver?
- What are his beliefs and values regarding money?
- What is his favorite money memory?

You can unearth some of these details with a little online sleuthing, but you're better served to just ask him directly, especially when it comes to credit scores. If he does not know the answer to these questions, you will need to consider this as well when deciding if he is an ideal partner for you. It should go without saying that if you are asking him these questions, you should be prepared to answer them as well.

It can be challenging to bring up credit scores naturally in conversation, but there are some natural triggers. If you're out together paying for something with a credit card, that gives you a fairly organic conversation opener, as do recent news stories on identity theft or fraud. If one of you is getting a new credit card, car, or house, or considering refinancing, that's the perfect time to bring up the topic of credit. It is extremely important to take advantage of this opportunity and learn about credit and explore what each of you value. Touch on your individual credit scores, but also make sure neither of you is carrying excessive debt. (Excessive being anything with high interest or debt for which you cannot afford the minimum monthly payments.)

There's always the chance that your ideal match might be a guy who has bad credit, doesn't pay bills on time, makes less money than you, or has a smaller net worth. It will make things tricky, but as long as you know and are comfortable with those factors, you can make the relationship work. You want to make sure financial disparities are not going to be a major issue in your relationship. To do this, you need to understand each other's credit and financial realities, including how it could impact your individual financial standing.

The list of topics to discuss won't necessarily lead to a fun or easy conversation, but it's an incredibly important one, especially if you're en-visioning a long-term future with this guy.

Before you become physically intimate with someone, you should be inquiring about their sexual health. Why wouldn't you also inquire about their financial health? That is, if this is someone you are looking at as a potential partner in life.

When should you have it? Well, that's really up to you. Trust your instincts as you move through the first few stages of dating someone, and don't dive in until your gut tells you the time is right. Consider your own personality and needs, your emotional boundaries, and the mind-set and personality of the person you're dating. In chapter 5, we discussed the stages of dating. Most people won't feel right digging into financial de-tails until stage 2. If your relationship is on a fast track, you might discuss money toward the end of stage 1, but any sooner may feel overwhelming or unnecessarily intense!

Regardless of when you bring it up, expect some awkwardness. It used to be that talking about sex was the most nerve-racking and sensitive conversation you'd have to navigate with a new partner, but now money is *much* more taboo. We live in an age when people feel perfectly comfortable sending photos of themselves—and sometimes their private parts—back and forth all the time. Despite increasingly relaxed attitudes around sex, we continue to be extremely reluctant to discuss money matters. (Side note: One guy stopped texting with me because I refused to send him photos of myself. I felt this was a risky move, he pushed the issue, and I broke it off. I knew what I wanted, and it wasn't someone so obsessed with looks.)

Your first talk about finances with a new partner can be a doozy, but that doesn't mean you should avoid it. You should be prepared. Sweeping financial concerns under the rug or ignoring them completely is just about the worst thing you can do in a relationship. It's a well-documented fact that money is the main topic that causes couples to fight. A Bankrate survey found that almost half of American couples argue over financial issues, and 60 percent do not like their partner's spending habits. April Davis's research produced similar findings, reporting that "over 70 percent of divorces have some sort of connection with money issues." There would probably be fewer money-centric fights if married couples worked out a solid communication plan ahead of time and spoke more freely about money. Planting the seed of that healthy precedent begins when you're still dating.

So, where do you start? Although I would *not* recommend asking questions about net worth, annual income, or tax returns on the first date, you definitely need to address them at some point. Again, trust your gut. Consider talking money on a night you're staying in together. Swapping credit scores in a busy restaurant can make people feel vulnerable. Preface the conversation by saying, "I know this may be a little awkward ..." and then explaining why discussing finances is important to you. Have the conversation in a setting that is relaxed and comfortable for both of you. It doesn't need to be a formal meeting, and it could even be while cooking together or shopping.

If he reacts badly to the very idea of revealing his financial details, consider what that signifies. Ask him to talk about why the topic is upsetting him or why he is reluctant to share. In a solid and equal partnership, both people should be unafraid of frank honesty. Think about how you might feel if he has had a bankruptcy or is required to pay child support or spousal maintenance. If your lives are going to intertwine, you need to know these things about each other.

Before you have the actual conversation, consider what to do if he reveals that he's a hot mess in the money department. What are your deal-breakers? How do you feel about someone who's drowning in debt? Where are you willing to compromise? Don't set any hard-and-fast rules, but prepare yourself emotionally for bad news. If someone is totally perfect for you in almost every way but turns out to be a walking financial disaster, you need to decide how you'll handle that.

If your potential partner has his own finances in good order, that's great! But make sure your first money conversation isn't also your last. It's easy to spend time and energy puzzling out the basics at the beginning and then get lazy and complacent as time goes by. Pay attention, plan together, and communicate frequently.

Do those things in your non-money life as well! Paying attention to your significant other is key to keeping a relationship thriving, but we often let it slide. When people stop paying attention to one another, they can drift apart. Think about it. When you first meet someone, he showers you with love, attention, and gifts. Over months or years, those signs of affection may subside or disappear completely. Why? We get comfortable, lazy, or disinterested. If you can keep yourself alert and engaged, you'll give your relationship a much better chance of long-term success.

Summary

You've worked hard to get where you are, and no one should be able to take that away from you. Making sure you are safe while you date—financially, emotionally, and physically—is absolutely essential. Craft exit strategies, make sure your own finances are in shipshape, and discuss money matters openly and honestly when the time is right.

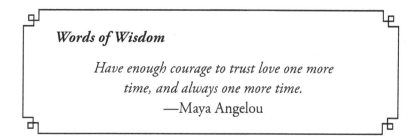

Words of Wisdom

Have enough courage to trust love one more time, and always one more time.
—Maya Angelou

8

It All Boils Down to Money

My worst date was with a millionaire. We went to dinner, and he ordered everything on the menu, then he insisted I read him the bill since he had forgotten his glasses. Toward the end of the night, he laid these charming lines on me: "Don't you know who I am?" "I deserve a kiss for riding in your piece-of-crap car," and finally, "How many more lonely nights do you want to endure?"

Self-Supporting Stacy

***

Still not convinced that discussing money matters openly with your potential partners is crucial? Then, let's dig a little deeper, shall we?

At each stage of your relationship, money concerns will surface in different ways. Is one of you extremely responsible with money—and the other is completely careless? Perhaps there is not enough money, too much money, or as a couple, you don't see eye to eye on how to handle your finances. Whether you're just getting to know each other or are envisioning your future together, money is an important consideration at all phases and stages of your relationship.

In this chapter, we will examine each of those stages and explore the pertinent money issues.

The Beginning

Although we've covered many of the money issues that arise at the very start of relationships in chapter 6 and chapter 7, here's a little recap:

- Who should pay for dinners? Drinks? Outings? At what point do you discuss how you'll share costs as you date?
- How do you handle it if one of you earns much more than the other?
- What if one of you chooses to date far outside your actual financial comfort zone? How can you be diplomatic in the face of this reality?
- When and how can you have "the money talk" with minimal awkwardness?

In this phase, you may still be hedging your bets and unsure if you'll commit, but even so, you must be mindful of how money figures into your dating life.

Be aware that you are setting precedents in this phase. If your boyfriend gives you flowers every Friday for the first six months, then suddenly stops, your dynamic might change. If you go out for happy hour every Tuesday at the beginning, consider how you feel if you suddenly can't. Don't create a financial picture of extravagance that doesn't align with your financial reality when you're in that first flush phase of romance. Whatever you do at the start should be sustainable in the long term.

Committed Dating

Once you've been together for several months or even a year, money priorities shift—and so do the money questions you'll be facing together.

- How will you handle gift-giving occasions? Would setting a dollar-amount cap be helpful?
- If one or both of you have children, how will you handle the purchasing of gifts for the kids?
- When you travel together, how will you divide costs?

- If you're traveling to visit one of your families, how does that impact sharing payments, if at all?
- Have you discussed long-term financial planning? Wills? Insurance? (Refer back to chapter 7 for more detail on these specific issues.)
- If either/both of you have children and go out to dinner as a family, who pays?
- What will you do if one of you wants to take an expensive vacation, but the other can't afford to pay for half of the costs?
- Do either of you have student loan debt? If so, how are you managing it?
- If you move in together eventually, how will you divide up living expenses?

You might not be quite ready to jump to the next phases of commitment, but you're no longer playing the field. And that means upping the ante when it comes to being honest about money matters.

Moving in Together

Once you move in together, the most pressing question that arises is how to divide expenses. It isn't quite as tricky if you are buying a place together or renting a space that you've picked out as a couple. If he is moving into your place or vice versa, you need to decide the best way to split costs—or make a plan for how the bills are going to get paid and decide who is in charge of what before those bills start to show up. Think about creating a cohabitation agreement.

Consider dividing costs by percentage of total income: If you make $180K, and he makes $95K, your total income is $275K. Your portion of that is about 66 percent, so you could consider paying 66 percent of rent/mortgage, any shared bills, groceries, etc. This can also be helpful if you need to furnish your place or make any substantial repairs.

Moving in together may also mean sharing a car or spending lots of time in one car or another. Some couples consider splitting gas and insurance costs to make things feel more equitable.

At this stage, you're probably not ready to fully merge your finances, but you'll have more shared costs than ever before. You need to decide how you'll handle dividing your expenses. There isn't just one way to accomplish this. What is important is that you both lay your cards out on the table while communicating openly and honestly about what each other needs, and how you will work together moving forward.

In this modern age, marriage isn't the only option for couples. It's vital that you have an open discussion about the pros and cons of marriage versus cohabitating as well as your reasons for both.

Being in love and wanting to spend your lives together does not necessarily translate into marriage being the right choice for you, from a financial perspective. As of the writing of this book, there is no longer a marriage tax penalty. There could be more tax benefits for married couples than singles.

There are many things to consider: Are either of you responsible for paying or are you receiving spousal maintenance? Are either of you required to pay child support? Are there any judgments or liens against your partner that could affect your finances?

It might be a little or very uncomfortable for you to discuss these matters with your partner, but it serves as a wonderful exercise of your ability to communicate and resolve situations. These premarital or pre-cohabitation conversations concerning finances are a window into how you and your partner can and will address other important issues that may arise during the course of your relationship.

An inability to discuss and resolve these agreements is a sign that this may not be the ideal match for you.

Engagement

Someone once asked me if it was true that a man should spend 5 percent of his income on an engagement ring. My response was that as a woman, I feel that if the man made $400,000 a year and only spent $20,000 on a ring, that is cheap. However, as a wealth advisor, I think that 5 percent is a very realistic percentage.

What is the correct amount to spend? There is no magic equation to answer that question. Many stick to the 5 percent rule or believe that three-to-six month's salary is a good ballpark, but ultimately, it comes down to what one can reasonably afford. You are going to fall in love with the ring regardless of the amount it costs because you love your partner. If you only want the ring because of its hefty price tag, you shouldn't be getting engaged at all. In fact, according to a study released by Andrew Francis and Hugo Mialon, professors in the Department of Economics at Emory University, the more a couple spends on an engagement ring and wedding ceremony, the shorter the marriage. The younger generation also believes with only spending what you can afford. In fact, according to a survey by TD Ameritrade, two-thirds of younger Americans – Generation Z and young millennials – think an engagement ring should cost less than $2,500.

Since this is always a hot topic, I looked to social media to gauge what others felt was the correct amount to spend. The responses I received from my colleagues, friends, and clients struck me as levelheaded and fair:

- Most people believed there was no specific amount/percentage that should be spent. Instead, they focused on picking a ring that the bride-to-be would love—one that fit her style *and* his budget.
- Nobody should be pressured to spend a certain dollar amount or adhere to a formula for price calculation. Spend what you can afford.
- The price of the ring shouldn't be what makes or breaks the engagement.

I would add that you shouldn't want or expect your significant other to take out a loan for your ring. If he can't afford the ring, how can both of you possibly afford the wedding or honeymoon? Will you need to buy a home? Are children in your budget? If you've got your heart set on a ring that's out of his (or your collective) price range right now, then wait. It's not a necessity. Consider buying a less costly ring for the time being or wearing a family heirloom that symbolizes love for both of you. Save up and buy your dream ring when you can pay for it in cash.

As you start to envision and plan your future life together, dedicate some time to exploring a few more aspects of your financial past. In fact, before you begin exploring the costs of your upcoming wedding, plan a conversation around these three key questions:

1. What are the three most important money lessons you learned growing up?
2. What are your three biggest money worries?
3. What are the three most important ways you want to use money to leave a legacy?

Before you merge your life and finances with another person, you need to have a solid understanding of how he (or she) thinks and feels about money in general terms. This will help you see where you share money values and where you diverge. This knowledge will help you build a budget, a retirement plan, and a shared fiscal life together that truly works for you both.

Why does this matter? Because even couples who think they're in alignment often aren't. Millennial newlyweds are doing a poor job of discussing their finances, which is creating stress and strain in their relationships according to Fidelity Investments' Couples and Money study.

- The study found that, while the majority of survey respondents said they are communicating about finances, one-third don't even know how much the other half of the couple makes, while one-seventh aren't even sure if their spouse is employed.
- Fidelity found that more than four in ten couples aren't in agreement about the age they want to retire. Meanwhile, 54 percent of survey respondents can't agree on how much they should save by the time they reach retirement age.

A survey by *Money* magazine found that 79 percent of millennials and 91 percent of boomers believe that they are in agreement with their partners on saving for retirement, but digging deeper reveals a different story. Of people who are married or living with a significant other, 10 percent of boomers and 40 percent of millennials have no idea what their partner's retirement account balance might be, while 14 percent of boomers and 40 percent of millennials aren't sure when their partners plan to retire.

This data is further supported by the Fidelity Investments' Couples and Money survey, which also found that:

- As for their financial documents, the survey revealed that, while a slight majority said they know their spouse's passwords to bank, credit card, social media, and investment accounts, about three in ten couples disagree on whether they provided the information to their spouse.

- Fidelity found in its latest survey of 1,662 couples with household incomes of $75,000 or more or at least $100,000 in investable assets that more than half of the couples said they carried debt into their marriage. For those that did, four in ten said it has had a negative impact.

- Among those that said they were concerned about debt, close to half of the respondents said that money is the biggest challenge in their relationship. Underscoring the importance of communication, Fidelity found that, of the couples that brought debt into the relationship, 49 percent contradict each other as to who has to pay off the debt, 55 percent think they are responsible for taking on the debt of their spouse, and 33 percent expect their partner to pay it off. Meanwhile, 67 percent of survey respondents said they fight about money, while 33 percent said they have difficulty talking about budgeting and spending.

These may sound like matters that can be hashed out along the way, but you're far better off getting them sorted out at the beginning. When you're not aligned from the start, you may end up with dwindling funds later in life.

One final word of advice for engaged women: If you're having serious doubts, trust your gut. Research conducted at Emory University shows that although men get "cold feet" more frequently, when *women* have pre-marriage apprehensions, the couple is twice as likely to eventually divorce.

> As you read through these stages and their associated money issues, which ones were the scariest to you? Why do you think that is? How can you be sure to address those issues with your partner in a way that feels genuine and safe to you?

Getting Married

Getting married for the first time comes with a whole boatload of pressures. Pressure to throw a big, flashy wedding. The pressure to take an expensive honeymoon or buy a house, even if you can't afford it. There is pressure to have kids, regardless of your financial situation.

Then there's the pressure to get married in the first place! It's huge and very real, but it's *totally manufactured*. Just because you're in a healthy, loving relationship doesn't mean that you must marry! If you'd rather keep your commitment between the two of you and leave city hall out of it, do it. The world is slowly becoming more accepting of varied relationship styles, so unless you're just dying to enjoy the tax benefits of an on-the-books marriage, feel free to skip it. Define your love and your relationship for yourselves.

Bear in mind, too, that marriage can have some financial *disadvantages*! If you're single and make $100K, you can contribute to a Roth IRA. If you marry someone who also makes $100K and file jointly, neither of you is eligible to contribute to a Roth. (I told this to two clients who've been engaged for nearly three years, and they decided on the spot to just scrap the wedding and stay engaged!) Of course, many couples want to honor their commitment to each other through a formal wedding. There's no doubt that planning a wedding can be a thrilling (if costly) experience!

There are entire websites and in-depth courses dedicated to planning and paying for a wedding, and that topic is simply beyond the scope of this book. Once you're engaged, you'll obviously have to start discussing wedding costs, including everything from the flowers and reception hall to the honeymoon. In this day and age, you can't just expect the bride's family to shell out for everything. (Many people don't even want that!) As you plan the details, be savvy about the costs. Keep in mind that the average American wedding costs more than $35K.[3] You get to decide if you'd rather sink that money into a single day of celebration or your future together. And couples who sink $20,000 or more into their wedding are 46 percent more likely to divorce, according to research from Emory University.

---

[3] The Knot, "The National Average Cost of a Wedding Hits $35,329," https://www. theknot.com/content/average-wedding-cost-2016. January 30, 2018.

Before the wedding day, you also need to decide if you want to merge your finances once you're married. You each have retirement accounts, checking, savings, and other assets as individuals. What are you going to pool together, and what (if anything) will be kept separate?

Couples can maintain their own accounts while also having joint accounts. There isn't one single system or setup that works perfectly for everyone. The most important thing is to figure out what feels best and works most efficiently for you as individuals *and* as a team. Here are a few different account setup variations that I suggest to my clients:

Joint

Some couples prefer to pool everything into shared accounts. Joint checking, savings, investments, credit cards, etc. Your Roth IRA, Traditional IRA, retirement plans through work, and 401(k) are individual retirement accounts, meaning they can only be in one person's name, but most of your other accounts can be merged. This will work only if you communicate with each other openly and constantly.

- Pros: Fewer accounts mean better consolidation, and pooling of resources encourages you to create shared financial goals.
- Cons: With multiple people drawing on shared accounts, you may not always know exact balances. This uncertainty creates a higher probability of overdrafts. Also, resentments can build if one party consistently spends more than the other.

Completely Separate

Another option is to keep all of your accounts 100 percent separate. You each have your own income, savings, checking, and retirement accounts, and they don't mingle.

- Pros: You know exactly where your money is and what it is spent on. You don't need to track one another's spending.
- Cons: Your allocation can suffer. You feel isolated in your own finances and less like a united and coordinated team.

Mixture

Many couples keep their own checking accounts, but also have a joint account where both contribute funds to pay shared bills and expenses.

No matter what you decide, make sure you're making the right choice for both you and your partner. Regardless of your account breakdown, it can be helpful to set a mutual spending cap. It could be $500 or $1,000 or whatever you decide upon. This means that neither of you can go out and spend that amount without first talking to your spouse about it, but also that purchases below the agreed-upon limit are fair game. If you're out shopping with girlfriends and find the perfect pair of shoes for $150, you can buy them without having to ask. It also means your partner can spring for a $200 weedwacker without getting your stamp of approval. This setup creates a helpful hybrid of autonomy and accountability. Just make sure you're truly comfortable with either of you making discretionary purchases that fall below your shared spending limit. You don't want to come home to discover that your spouse has bought a new toy that's well within budget and end up feeling resentful about it. Be honest and open when choosing your limit. A Fidelity survey found that 38 percent of money arguments don't end up being resolved in a way that makes both people happy. Don't let your marriage become a part of that statistic!

It's essential to discuss insurance costs as you begin your marriage too. If you both have access to employer-subsidized insurance, you'll need to investigate whose is a better value and fit for your needs and then examine how to handle the out-of-pocket portion. If one or both of you is self-employed, discuss your options in-depth.

As a newly married couple in the modern world, you'll likely have very different financial priorities than your parents or grandparents. Years ago, I'd urge my newlyweds to start saving for retirement right away, but now I end up advising them to pay down their student loan and credit card debt instead. I also tell them they can wait to buy a house until some of that debt is erased. There's no hurry—no matter what your friends and family say!

Not long ago, I met with a young couple who planned to move back to Minnesota from where they'd met in Arizona. Very wisely, they wanted to understand the costs and advantages of this move. The wife was pregnant, and they knew they'd rather raise their kids in the Twin Cities, where the school system was stronger, but they also knew that cost of living was higher in suburban Minneapolis than it had been in Arizona. I advised them to not focus on their Roth IRAs right now since they'd need more liquid money to cover moving and baby costs. Also, I encouraged them to rent for a few years until they were settled, more stable, and able to buy a home from a stronger financial position.

Marriage comes with a boatload of pressures. Hopefully I've given you the information you need to push back against some of them!

Having Kids

Once you're married and your financial situation as a couple is on an even keel, you may begin to consider having kids together. Even if you're not married, you may be mulling the prospect of parenthood. Regardless of your status—married or single—you should remember that having children is a costly choice. A middle-income, married couple is estimated to spend $284,570 to raise a single child born in 2018, according to a report by the Department of Agriculture. In my years as a wealth advisor, I've determined that it costs far more than that. I would say it costs well over $1 million to raise a child from birth until age eighteen, when you factor in medical care, activities, clothes, school costs, etc.

Just think about how much health insurance costs each month. When kids enter the picture, you'll be paying another $200–400 a month that you weren't spending before. Then consider after-school activities, sports equipment, education, and additional costs. Absolutely nothing compares to the joy of raising children of your own, while watching them grow and thrive. Remember that considering the financial implications is absolutely essential.

Before you dive into parenthood, reflect on the following questions to determine if you are truly ready to make the leap. Are you free of excess debt? Determine how much debt you and your spouse have accumulated, come up with a plan, and set a goal date to get that debt completely paid off. Once it is gone, you can begin aggressively saving for your growing family.

Have major career and income decisions been made? Budgeting and saving money can be difficult in itself, so remember that costs associated with a new child represent additional expenses on top of your standing monthly bills. You will need to determine if your goal is to maintain a dual-income household or attempt to live off a single income. You will also want to come up with a plan of action for maternity or paternity leave. Can you meet all of your financial obligations if both you and your spouse take time off?

Do you have adequate health insurance coverage? Even if you have health insurance, the costs for prenatal, maternity, and postnatal care can be staggering. Depending on your health insurance coverage, unforeseen circumstances like a cesarean section or an extended hospital stay can present new parents with hefty hospital bills. Investigate your coverage—and keep an eye out for any holes.

Are baby clothes covered? Infants grow incredibly fast, and new parents need to be careful about clothing costs. Many outfits you purchase may only fit for a single month! Before you bring home your baby, create a game plan that involves a near-constant influx of secondhand baby clothes from consignment stores and family hand-me-downs.

Does your budget have room for child care? Child care is a very large, ongoing expense for many working parents. You can choose to avoid this expense by having one parent stay at home, but most modern households are dual-income households. Assessing how child care will be handled and paid for in advance will help you prepare and budget.

Are you able to save for college? Many parents still choose to help pay for their children's college educations, at least to some extent. According to the College Board, the average cost of tuition and fees for the 2018–2019 school year was $35,830 at private colleges, $10,230 for state residents at public colleges, and $26,290 for out-of-state residents attending public universities. Over the past decade, expenses at public institutions have increased nearly 40 percent, and costs will almost certainly continue to rise. In light of this, most couples begin saving college money before their kids are even born! However, before you start socking away tuition money, make sure you are maxing out your contributions to your own retirement plans.

Plenty of couples get pregnant before considering these questions, but they often scramble to get by financially. Enjoy the excitement and romance of planning your family, but be sure to keep money matters in mind as you do so.

Blended Family Basics

Information from the most recent Vital Statistics Report shows that about 75 percent of divorced persons eventually remarry, and about 65 percent of remarriages involve children from a prior marriage.[4] More divorces and remarriages mean that blended families are becoming more prevalent. And when existing families merge, questions always arise around finances, shared expenses, and division of fiscal responsibilities.

A client told me a story about a friend of hers whose blended family ran into trouble around Christmastime. This woman had a teenage daughter from a previous marriage, and her ex had never paid a dime in child support. In fact, she constantly fielded calls from collections agencies looking for him! She remarried, and she and her new husband had a son together. As the family is opening Christmas gifts, the teenage daughter sees that a giant box is addressed to her, from Deadbeat Dad. Inside are giant stuffed Mickey and Minnie dolls, and a note saying he's taking her to Disneyworld. Now, Mom and Stepdad had been planning to take both kids on a ski trip as their big holiday gift to the family, but they hadn't announced the plan yet. Mom finds herself in a pickle. Does she forbid her daughter from going to Disney and insist she ski instead? Does she let the daughter go with Deadbeat Dad and risk disappointing her young son? A big question that remained was just where the heck he got the money for the trip anyway.

There seems to be endless advice for parents, but far less for stepparents and blended households. This mom is likely stumped as to how to handle her situation because nobody talks about this stuff!

My advice to her would be to remember that this isn't about her—it's about her daughter, who is probably ecstatic about her dad's sudden burst of generosity. It shouldn't matter where the money came from, so just let that go. If Deadbeat Dad suddenly wants to be around, support that change, even if it shifts the family dynamic. Do your best to forget your own frustrations with your ex and celebrate how special it makes your daughter feel to finally get some love and attention from him. That's more important in the long run.

---

[4] CDC (National Center for Health Statistics) Homepage. http://www.cdc.gov/nchs/. January 30, 2018.

I'd also remind her that she can take her son skiing another time. Handling the situation this way might spark some jealousy, but it also creates an opportunity to educate the kids about timing and budgets. It's also a teachable moment about how life can feel wildly unfair sometimes!

Many of the blended families I work with choose to keep their finances separate, but some prefer to merge their finances. There are advantages to both choices, though merged finances can become tricky when there are multiple children at various ages and an unequal financial situation.

Here are some ideas to ponder if you're combining your family with another:

- If you or your partner have child support payments, how will that impact your collective budget?
- Are you more comfortable handling all of your own children's expenses? Splitting them all? Sharing some and handling others yourself? If you all go out to a dinner as a family, who pays? When you travel, who picks up the bill? When it comes to buying books, school supplies, and team uniforms, do you help all kids or is each parent responsible for her/his own?
- How will you handle college costs?

I have two kids of my own and, regardless of who I might date or marry in the future, I have every intention of paying for all of their needs and expenses myself. I stick to an "I'll-pay-for-mine-and-you-pay-for-yours" philosophy when it comes to blended family finances. Having said that, my policy doesn't work for everyone. Each family situation is unique.

I work with a couple who have been married for about twelve years and merged their families. The woman has two kids from a previous marriage, and their biological dad has done virtually nothing to support them. She put away as much as she could for their college costs, but it wasn't enough to cover everything. Her youngest child's dad is her second husband, and he's able to fully fund this son's college. Knowing this would be the case, he also helped supplement the money she put toward his step-kids' college costs.

When all kids are treated as mutual kids, things tend to run smoother. I still insist on paying all of my own kids' expenses, but after working with hundreds of blended families over the years, I can see how effective it can be to consider everyone as full-blood relatives. Fund sports equipment, private school costs, medical costs, vacations, everything the kids need, step- or otherwise. The number of arguments and hurt feelings is drastically reduced when everyone feels equal. Of course, everyone has to be on board and totally comfortable with this agreement; otherwise, it simply won't work.

On the flipside, covering costs for your step-kids can backfire if your relationship with their parent dissolves. Say you marry someone whose kids are older than yours and need more money up front, so you make sure they're fully funded. If you end up divorcing or separating, will you be able to do the same for your own, younger kids when they come of age? If not, you'll be in deep trouble. That is why I recommend looking after your own children's needs first and then considering the needs of the blended family.

A prenuptial agreement can help clarify financial issues in blended families, especially if there are kids or a business involved. You want to protect yourself and your children financially, while also creating a shared setup that feels fair and equitable. Keep an open mind as you discuss your options and create a plan that works for you, your spouse, and all the children.

Getting Divorced

Divorce and money are inextricably linked. No matter how extravagantly or modestly you and your ex tried to be in your shared life, separating shines a light on your fiscal truth. Divorce can put you on the receiving end of a startling wake-up call about your true financial situation. (Side note: A typical divorce costs between $15K and $25K, which is about as much as a typical wedding![5]) Labor economists have noted that divorced women of all ages have the highest poverty rates in the United States, so clearly getting divorced can have massive financial repercussions.

I know a fantastic woman who married a pro athlete, and throughout their marriage, her life revolved around entertaining his teammates and their families, managing press appearances, and meeting all of his career

---

[5] Bankrate, "How much does divorce cost"? https://www.bankrate.com/personal-finance/smart-money/how-much-does-divorce-cost/, January 30, 2018.

needs. Eventually he retired, but even after he stopped playing and bringing in a massive salary, they continued to live the lifestyle. They'd gotten used to a certain standard of living, and neither was prepared to pare down and budget wisely. In fact, she paid no attention at all to their finances.

Until he asked for a divorce.

That's when she came to me, and we both found out what was going on behind the scenes. It turns out her husband had been spending far beyond their means (which he claimed he did to try to keep her happy and keep their relationship stable). I had the unhappy task of telling her she needed to get a job, and fast. I had to explain that she didn't have the money or credit to buy a house and would have to rent. After living like a wealthy wife for decades, she suddenly had to manage as a middle-income single gal.

You don't have to receive divorce papers from a pro athlete to end up in a similar situation. Since most couples fail to be honest, open, and communicative about money *during* their marriages, many end up totally shocked by their financial situations once a divorce is in process.

That said, being financially savvy in the midst of a divorce doesn't have to be complex. In fact, there are just four essential things that you will need to survive divorce: a place to live, little or no debt, retirement assets, and liquid money. And the goal is to have a balance of each of these four things:

Place to Live

A married couple is able to exclude up to $500,000 of gains, and a single person is able to exclude up to $250,000 of gains on the sale of a home as long one or both of you have occupied that house for two out of the last five years. Depending on the divorce, it may be advantageous for one spouse to take the home, while in another situation, it could be financially disastrous for that same spouse to take the home. A house is not a liquid asset and may have less appreciation potential compared with money set aside for retirement. And there's nothing wrong with renting for a period of time.

Regardless of who takes the house—or if you mutually agree to sell—you will need a place to stay that is affordable and accommodates your needs. Crashing with family members should be a temporary stopgap. Do your best to find stable housing for yourself and your family as soon as it becomes clear that a divorce is imminent.

Little or No Debt

There is a high cost to carrying debt, so be careful about using credit to protect your assets and your future. When divorce becomes inevitable, assess your debt load and manage it actively. If you or your spouse have credit cards that carry a balance, pay them down aggressively. If you have cards with a zero balance, call and cancel them. Creditors will want the debt paid regardless of your marital situation. If your spouse opens a credit card with your name on it and does not pay that debt, the creditor has every right to come after you.

Retirement Assets

Retirement assets can be varied and complex, so make sure that you do not forget about smaller or less active accounts and leave money on the table. If you receive retirement assets from your spouse's 401(k) plan, you may need a Qualified Domestic Relations Order (QDRO) to separate those assets. The QDRO is a legal document that is different from your divorce decree. It is sent to the benefits department of the 401(k) plan provider to delineate how assets should be divided. Make sure the QDRO is written correctly *before* the divorce is final to ensure that you receive your retirement assets.

Bear in mind, though, that some benefit plans cannot be divided. In this case, you should negotiate dividing other assets from the marriage instead. For example, if a pension cannot be divided, take more 401(k) assets from your former spouse. If you have the option of taking a Traditional IRA or a 401(k), take the Traditional IRA. It doesn't cost anything to transfer and you don't need a QDRO, just a divorce decree and your signature on a few forms.

Liquid Money

Liquid money is not in your 401(k), tied up in a CD, or stuffed under your mattress. It is six to twelve months of income set aside for emergencies, preferably in a money market account. A money market account is similar to a savings account, but it has the potential to earn more interest. The important thing is to make sure it is an insured money market account. The FDIC insures up to $250K automatically, but some firms (like the one I am partnered with) insure above $1 million. Having access to a comfortable amount of liquid money throughout your divorce will help you feel sane and secure.

Many people mistakenly believe that divorce is a single event. In reality, there are three distinct phases within the divorce process: the beginning of the divorce, the middle of the divorce, and after the divorce. In each of these stages, you will have different financial needs, though you should have liquid money available at all times. In the beginning, you will need liquid money for the retainer to hire an attorney. Consider putting this liquid money in a money market account rather than a savings or checking account so you can potentially earn more interest on it. (But make sure you understand what a money market account is, and what it can do for you!) In the middle stage, you'll need liquid money for unexpected expenses. After the divorce, liquid money is important because you are on your own and need to be prepared in case of an emergency.

As you navigate your divorce, you should strive for a balance of each of these four things: You need a mix of a little from each category, not an abundance of one category and none in the others. And above all, educate yourself, get organized, and ask for help when you need it.

Now let's take a moment to acknowledge how truly awful divorce can be. More often than not, it brings out the vindictive, petty, obstinate parts of everyone's personalities, and hurtful things are said. Unfortunately, amicable divorces are rare. I know from personal experience that a contentious divorce is a draining experience. You don't always see someone's true colors until you try to divorce them.

Next, let's talk about how utterly gratifying *life after divorce* can be. A huge reason why I chose to write this book is that there's a real lack of supportive, realistic, heartfelt advice for divorced women. I want to remind all you delightful divorcées that the new life you're forging for yourself can be a fantastic one! Divorce is horrendous when you're in the thick of it, but when you're on the other side, you'll thrive. I believe most divorced women do. If they're business owners, their businesses can flourish. If they're moms, they're caretaker load may decrease drastically. (We all know that two kids and a husband often feels like *three* kids.) If they've put their hobbies aside for the sake of the relationship, they reclaim them with eager enthusiasm. And many of them realize that they don't need a partner to live a fulfilling life—and that realization is freeing. Divorce gives us permission to do all the things we've secretly longed to do, but that marriage made impossible.

Several years ago, I watched a client rebuild her life and reclaim her independence after a divorce. During the mediation process, she fretted about her ex holding up his end. Would he pay child support? Would he pitch in for the kids' expenses? Knowing that she was a capable entrepreneur with a dormant business waiting to be revived, I sat her down and said, "Look, these are *your* kids. Just take care of them. If you need more money, go make it yourself."

She told me that conversation transformed her perspective. She stopped looking to her ex for money, and she started focusing on earning more herself. We can't control what someone else will or won't do, but we have total control over what we decide to do and make happen.

Of course, some women don't have the leverage to do this. If you've been a stay-at-home mom for decades, your earning potential may have taken a hit. If you're working in a field that has limited opportunities, doubling your income might be a fantasy. This isn't to say that every divorced woman should expect to go it alone and pay for everything her entire family needs forever! The point is to adopt a self-sufficient mentality wherever and however you can, partner with your ex when it makes sense, and find your own solutions when it doesn't. Doing so will make your post-divorce life easier, better, and happier.

Speaking of crafting a happier postdivorce life, here's my number one piece of advice for divorced women: *Don't get remarried.* (Or if you have to, at least sign a prenup!) We think of marriage as an achievement, a box to be checked, a socially important status to achieve. In truth, it really isn't. You got divorced for a reason, so spend time honoring and exploring that reason before you decide you want to marry again. Divorced women often navigate the world as single moms, which means they're balancing careers, kids, extended families, social lives, and their own health, hobbies, travel, and more. Trying to wedge a new relationship into that equation can be more trouble than it's worth. Focus on yourself. Focus on your family. Date, have fun, live your life, but don't decide that you absolutely must be married in order to be a complete, fulfilled adult.

Because, take it from me, you don't.

Advice for Widows

Losing a spouse is one of the most difficult things anyone can experience. I've worked with dozens of men and women struggling to make sense of their lives after their partners have died. I've seen firsthand how devastating this loss can be. I've also seen firsthand how many smart, capable, savvy women have spent their entire lives deferring to their spouses on financial matters. Suddenly, in the wake of their spouses' deaths, they struggle to exercise basic financial common sense.

When women become widows, we tend to dwell on the things we wish we could've done and the conversations we should've had to prepare for this unexpected (and unwanted) independence. No one wants to think about a spouse dying, but avoiding those challenging discussions inevitably leads to regret, *especially* around money. New widows face total despair and turmoil, and when they have no idea whether they'll receive a life insurance payout or not, that just adds to their already staggering emotional burden.

A few years back, I met with a woman whose husband had become terminally ill. It wasn't until he was diagnosed that she began to think about what her life might be like without him, and by that time, it was too late to buy any additional life insurance or do anything beyond preparing as best she could. When her husband passed, she became severely depressed, gained a lot of weight, and struggled to rebuild her life.

For years afterward, she had a run of false starts. She'd try to relaunch her business, join a gym, and start to climb her way out—and then she would suffer some sort of setback and end up feeling stuck, lost, and miserable again. It took her five years to get back to earning a steady income and feeling fully confident. She was fortunate to have life insurance money to scrape by for those years, but we spoke many times about how she needed to think about her future more thoroughly. I reminded her that she needed to consider potentially catastrophic outcomes to avoid being caught off guard by her circumstances again. I emphasized to her that understanding her financial situation would give her more stability, control, and confidence. Today, we've got a solid plan in place for her in case she has to cope with any other losses.

The death of a spouse can be devastating and emotionally paralyzing at first, but it's important to make decisions and move ahead. Here are some tips that can help you stay smart in the midst of this tragic situation.

What to do as Soon as Possible

Get Organized

Meet with a wealth advisor to assess your situation. This professional can help in two major ways. First, it's difficult to make rational money decisions alone in times of extreme stress. Your wealth advisor can serve as an objective guide. Second, decisions about what to do with life insurance benefits, investments, retirement accounts, and your home have major tax, estate, and investment consequences. You'll need professional input before making changes or signing off on final decisions.

Continue Health Care Coverage

Don't let coverage lapse for yourself or your children. If your health insurance coverage was through your loved one's workplace, contact his or her employer within thirty days of their death.

Apply for Death, Disability, or Income Benefits

First, determine which benefits you are eligible for by touching base with your local Social Security office. You can also visit www.ssa.gov. Be sure to sign up for any coverage that is appropriate. If your spouse was eligible for a pension through their employer, investigate how to access it. It's better to get this process in motion as soon as possible.

Don't Focus on Paying Off the Mortgage

It's often tempting to pay off an existing mortgage or even pay cash for a new home, particularly when resources such as life insurance benefits become available. However, as long as interest rates remain low, it's sometimes better to keep the money in more liquid investments than tie it up in a residence.

Retitle Assets

Make sure to get the title changed on assets including real estate, cars, and other property held jointly with right of survivorship as well as joint bank, mutual fund, and brokerage accounts.

What to do in the Coming Weeks and Months

Don't Let Emotions Rule Financial Decisions

As you go through the grieving process, it is imperative that you be conscious of your shifting emotions—anger, sadness, hopelessness, denial, depression—and not let them influence your financial decisions. Don't be ashamed to ask for help whenever you need it.

Organize Financial Records

You've already done some of this work by collecting records to apply for death, disability, or pension benefits. Now collect the rest of your financial records, including statements for investment and retirement accounts, vehicle titles, deeds, bank accounts, credit cards, and other debt statements. Doing this will help you determine which assets you still have as well as identify any debts that are owed.

Transfer Ownership

You'll want to transfer ownership to your name only for all financial relationships you've held jointly. This includes bank accounts, investment accounts, loans, mortgages, automobiles, utilities, and so on.

Contact Creditors

You may find yourself temporarily unable to meet certain financial obligations. Contact creditors as soon as possible to explain the situation. Many may be willing to delay or even renegotiate payments.

Review Your Estate

Establish a new power of attorney and health care directive and review your will or trust documents. Refer back to chapter 7 for more details on estate planning.

What to do in the Near Future

Settle the Estate

Generally, you have nine months from the date of death of your loved one in which to settle their estate. Working with your wealth advisor and estate-planning attorney, review the will and other estate documents and handle any legal aspects of the settlement.

If you've received a sizable life insurance payout, it can be tempting to sock it away all at once. I've met with many widows who've said, "I've suddenly got $1 million. What on earth do I do with it?" I work with them to develop a plan to use the money incrementally and strategically. If they're behind on their retirement savings, we put a chunk into a Roth IRA. If there's debt, it gets paid off. Being that you don't pay taxes on life insurance money, it can be helpful to use it slowly over time instead of tying it up in one or two big investments!

Make Your Own Life Plans

In time, you'll begin to think about your own future. That means taking a long-term financial view. After you have regained some control of your life—and your financial life in particular—consider readjusting your investment portfolio so it's tailored to your goals and needs for the long term.

I worked with a forty-year-old widow who tragically lost her husband and ended up with an enormous life insurance payout. She became the sole parent to their five-year-old son and was stunned by her new circumstances. All of her friends said, "Just be done! You don't need to work anymore, so why make yourself? Retire early." She resisted this advice.

"Why should I act like *everything* in my life is over?" she said. "I mean, emotionally I'll never be quite the same, but I don't want to put my career and personal development on indefinite hold."

She spent a year with her son, recouping and reevaluating. When he was old enough to attend all-day school and the noncompete clause from her previous job had expired, she launched a new business. It was an idea she'd been nurturing for years but never had the courage to pursue. Now, just a few years after launch, she's bringing in $1 million or more in revenue each year. She's happier and more fulfilled than she *ever* thought she could be after her loss.

If my advice sounds cold or heartless, pause for a moment to consider what your departed spouse would want for you in his (or her) absence. Endless sadness, stagnation, and eventual financial ruin? Not a chance! Even without them, our loved ones would want us to be safe, secure, and yes, even happy.

So, if your partner or husband dies, allow yourself to mourn and recover and cope, but try not to adopt the mentality that your life is simply over. Give yourself a year. Settle your affairs before you even *consider* beginning to date. Don't jump into a new relationship too quickly, which so many widows do. Accept that in your own time, you *can* allow yourself to grow and learn and even love again.

Once you find a new partner, be open and communicate with that person. Be prepared and allow yourselves to consider worst-case scenarios together. The biggest issue that widows struggle with is lacking confidence around money matters. So many women take a hands-off approach and let their husbands handle the finances. If that husband is suddenly gone, they feel overwhelmed and lost. Women are smarter and more financially savvy than we realize. While losing a loved one is absolutely crushing, it can also help us realize that we must stay on top of our finances—no matter what.

Getting Remarried

Marrying again after divorcing or losing a spouse is an emotionally complex process, and it is different for everyone, but there are some common threads in every remarriage, especially when it comes to money.

Decide if you want to merge your finances or keep them separate. Again, there are pros and cons to both. Refer back to the "Getting Married" section in this chapter to review the basic ways to manage joint money. Choose an option that works for your specific financial situation.

Create a budget together. Whether a marriage is your first, second, or fifteenth, you're likely to move in together and have shared expenses. That means you need to sit down and hammer out a monthly budget that covers your costs and leaves room for savings. In the Resources section of this book, you will find our budget worksheet. Use it to start tracking where you spend your money. That is the easiest way to develop your budget.

Get a financial plan in place. Meet with a wealth advisor and discuss how to manage your individual and collective money for the long term. Sitting down with someone can help you both determine what your financial goals and plans should be.

Have investments in your own name. It can be tempting to make everything shared, especially if you're head over heels in love, but it's always wise to keep a few things separate. Feel free to make joint investments—but select a few for yourself. Since IRAs and retirement accounts can only be in one person's name, they are both easy options. Just because you get remarried doesn't mean you should stop saving for your own retirement.

Have a trust/estate plan. Refer back to chapter 7 for more on this topic.

These steps are important for any newly married couple, no matter their age or stage of life, but overlooking them in a second or third marriage can lead to disaster. Keep them in mind if you're on the road to getting married again.

Remember that you don't have to get remarried. Marriages to divorced men are less likely to last, according to US Census data. Although divorce rates are generally in decline, they've doubled for people over age fifty over the past two decades. Social media and dating websites make it easier to find new partners, but they also offer us an amazing tool for staying connected with friends and family, and for cultivating non-romantic relationships, many of which can be just as rewarding. If you're happy as a single person, honor that.

As you can see, money always matters! You may have gone out on five dates or fifty, you may just be getting to know each other or preparing to part ways ... no matter what phase you're in, it's essential to keep money top of mind. Doing so and advocating for your financial well-being will help your relationship remain healthy while helping you remain stable and protected.

Summary

Each relationship stage has its own unique financial challenges, but there isn't a single one that's entirely free of money-related concerns. Make sure you know which discussions need to be had at which milestones in your relationship.

Words of Wisdom

*A woman can always tell if a man loves her by
how much time he's willing to invest. Money spent
is meaningless, but time spent is priceless.*
—Tony A. Gaskins, Jr.

9

Money Questions for
Committed Couples

A long time ago, I was dating a married man. He told me again and again that he wanted to leave his wife, but he couldn't because they were drowning in debt. I was (and still am) extremely successful, so I figured there was a simple solution to this problem. I paid off his second mortgage and his credit cards. I even sprung for a nice Rolex for an "engagement" gift, assuming he'd make good on his promise, leave his wife, and propose to me. Not long after, when it became clear that no divorce was imminent, he explained that his life was less stressful now that the debts were erased, and he really had no reason to break up his marriage. Clearly, I should've dug deeper into how he'd racked up all that debt to begin with ... and questioned the wisdom of dating a married man who wasn't ready to commit right away.

Betty the Bachelorette

***

When people think of "dating," most imagine the beginning stages: picking out a flattering OkCupid profile photo or negotiating awkward blind dates. In reality, dating can stretch well beyond that flirty, exciting first phase. Everything up to (and even beyond) getting engaged still qualifies as "dating"! That means the months after you've committed to just one person still constitute a chapter in your love life that should be handled with care.

Let's say you've been with a guy for nine months, a year, or even three or more years. You're starting to wonder about taking it to the next level of commitment. It's been long enough, right? Coming up on time to have *the* talk?

That talk is frequently about whether you're ready to be exclusive—or possibly about whose apartment you should move into. It's seldom about understanding each other's financial status or situations. If you're on the brink of merging households—even if marriage isn't even on the table yet—I'd urge you to have a frank discussion about money. It's definitely important to know if the person you're about to move in with or commit to is up to his eyeballs in debt. It is equally important to find out if he's got a boatload of cash sitting under a mattress earning zero interest. If you are taking the next step in a relationship, it is imperative to understand your partner's financial risks and strengths. Too many couples don't talk about money early in their relationship, which ends up hurting them in the long run.

In the beginning, no one wants to take that first step of dipping a toe into the pool. It feels incredibly vulnerable to dive in, swim out to the deep end, and bare your fiscal soul—from credit to retirement to money memories to debt load to goals and fears about money. Most people are so emotionally embedded about their own financial situations that they don't want to face reality or share the gory details. It's kind of like stepping on the scale. You need to find out how much you weigh to know your starting point. If you weigh 175 but aren't happy with that number, you need to set a goal and decide where you are headed. If your ideal weight is 155, then you know how far you've got to go to reach your goal. With both weight loss and financial savvy, if you share your goal with someone else, he or she can help you accomplish it and keep you accountable along the way.

Talking about money doesn't have to be scary or intimidating! If you approach the topic with care, honesty, and a desire to do what's best for both you and your partner, discussing money matters will help you solidify your mutual trust.

So how do you *start* the conversation about money? Don't just sit down one day and say, "We need to talk." Instead, set a money date, plan a stay-cation, or even designate some time on your next trip together to have some deep conversations about goals, dreams, and individual financial situations. Find a quiet space, sit down with your partner, and prepare to take a fun journey. This journey will help you forge a better understanding of your own finances and gain an understanding of your partner's situation. You are building a foundation from which your lives will expand. You both need to know what it's made of.

Some difficult topics or upsetting money memories may be hard to discuss, but don't shy away from them. It is important to have a strong foundation for your relationship. Being open about money and personal goals will help create the strong foundation you will need to weather a lifetime together. If he is your "perfect match," he will accept and support you no matter what your finances may look like.

As you prepare to discuss money matters, here are some questions to help break the ice and get you rolling:

Money Values

1. What is your favorite money memory?
2. Are you a spender or a saver and why?
3. If you could change one thing about your financial situation, what would it be?
4. How much is in your savings account? Investment account?
5. Is there anything you are saving money for right now?
6. Where do you want to be in one year? Five years? Ten years? Twenty years?
7. Can we discuss setting a dollar amount that neither of us would spend without consulting the other?
8. How did your family discuss or handle money matters?
9. Are you a millionaire? Do you want to be? Why or why not?
10. Does money make you happy? Why or why not?
11. How will we keep things equal? What if you spend $100 and I spend $1,000 on an anniversary gift? Will this matter?
12. How much money do you donate each year? Which organizations, people, or things top your donation list? Why are they important to you?
13. Do you love your job?
14. Would you keep working the same job even if you didn't get paid?

15. What are the next two items on your Live It List™, and how will you pay for them?
16. If we were to get married, would we sign prenups?
17. If you won $10,000, what would you do with your winnings?
18. If you were given two years left to live, what if any changes would you make in your life?

Cash Flow

1. If an unexpected expense of $10,000 came up, how would you cover that expense?
2. How much do you have in your checking account? Do you balance your checking account? Why or why not?
3. How much income do you make? Are you W-2 or 1099?
4. Can you make it month to month on your current income? If not, what are you doing about it?
5. What do you spend too much on each month?
6. Do you have a budget? If you don't, would you be willing to create one?
7. How much money on average do you have left after your monthly expenses?

Retirement

1. How much do you have saved for retirement?
2. How much do you save for retirement each month, and where do you put it?
3. At what age do you want to retire? How much income do you want to have available on a monthly basis when you stop working?
4. Are you on track to meet your retirement savings goals? If not, what are you doing about it?
5. Do you have life insurance? If so, how much? What kind?
6. Do you have a will? A trust? What do they say?
7. Do you have a Roth IRA? Why or why not? Do you qualify to add to the Roth IRA?

8. Do you have company stock? Is it more than 5 percent of your net worth? Why or why not?
9. Do you think you are going to inherit money?
10. If you could afford to retire tomorrow, would you?

Assets

1. How much is your home worth? How much do you owe on your mortgage? What is the interest rate? How many years remain on your loan?
2. How is the value of your automobile? Do you have a loan on it? What is the interest rate? How much time is left on your loan?
3. What other assets do you have? What other assets do you want to accumulate?
4. Do you own a business? If so, how is it set up? What are your plans for your company? What is your day-to-day routine like?
5. If you don't own a business, would you ever want to start one?
6. What is your favorite asset?
7. What is the next asset you want to buy? How? When?

Children

1. Do you have college accounts set up for your kids? If so, what type and how much?
2. If we merge our lives together, will we share our kids' expenses? Including college?
3. How do you teach your kids about money?
4. Do you give your kids an allowance? How much? What do they use it for? Do they do any chores or meet any academic standards before they receive it?
5. Do you have a family 401(k)? Why or why not?
6. What is one thing you've learned about money that you wish you'd known as a kid?
7. Have you done a "wants-versus-needs" chart with your kids?
8. When do you pay for things for your kids? When do you make them pay for them?

Net Worth

1. What is your net worth? List all your assets and liabilities.
2. Did your parents talk to you about money?
3. If you won $1,000,000 in the lottery, what would you do with it?
4. Do you spend time with people who have a greater net worth than you? Why or why not?
5. Are you taking steps to increase your net worth?

Credit

1. What is your credit score?
2. Do you have credit card debt? If not, when was it last paid off?
3. When was the last time you were late paying a bill? Why?
4. Do you have any bad debt? If so, what is your plan to get rid of it?
5. What are your thoughts and feelings about debt?

As you discuss these questions and share your own answers, remember to reserve judgment as much as possible until you've heard the whole story. If it turns out your partner has a massive debt load, but it's due to family medical expenses, that's a different matter than racking up a crushing Visa bill on vacations and football tickets. Listen openly and make sure you've got all the facts before making up your mind. You may unearth something that turns out to be a deal-breaker, and you need to be prepared to handle that, but since you've already been together for many months, you should also be willing to offer support and help if he needs it.

And vice versa! It can be hard to predict what will trigger your partner's money panic, and something you reveal may set him off. Be honest and open about your history and situation, and if you've had some hiccups yourself, ask for his support. Within reason of course. You can't expect him to pay off your debts or offer to be the sole income earner. You *can* expect him to offer ideas and suggestions or just listen. If he isn't willing to offer support in those simple ways, that may show you that you're not so compatible after all.

> If you're not willing to be authentic about
> money early in your relationship, why would you
> expect honesty and transparency to be easy later?

Seven Key Questions

I believe you must know seven things about your partner's finances at a minimum. Most of them should be well covered by the sets of questions above, but just in case any get overlooked, I want to call them out here. When you are in a partnership, that means complementing each other's strengths as well as being on the same page moving forward together. If nothing else, make sure you know these seven things about your partner's finances:

His Credit Score

Everyone's credit score is connected to their Social Security number. Your score can be affected by your partner's score once you get married. If you have great credit and marry someone with horrible credit, this can hurt you. You can get a credit report for free at www.annualcreditreport.com, though you'll have to pay a fee to see your credit score.

How Much He Owes

You don't want to move in with someone only to find out that he's filed for bankruptcy or is in debt over his head and can barely make his minimum payments. You don't want to buy a house or car together and be shocked when you find out your partner can't afford his share. If either of you has children already, be certain to address child support and obligations. Do you expect your new partner to help you with those expenses? Or if he pays child support, how much does he pay, and will he need your help? Are his payments current? If he's divorced, does he pay spousal maintenance? These are some tough but important questions, and you need to know the answers.

How Much He Makes

You need to know this so you can plan for taxes, retirement, insurance, etc. It's not because you are nosy or eager to compete with him. You just need to know the lay of the land! His salary may impact your financial situation and plan if you decide to marry. If you partner with a man who makes $100,000 and you also make $100,000, you can contribute to your individual Roth IRA's while single, but once you marry and file a joint tax return, you will no longer qualify because you make too much money.

How Much He Saves

If you get in a relationship with someone who spends more than he makes and has nothing left to save, that's very telling. If you value saving, this could cause huge problems.

How Much He Spends and Why

Ask to see his monthly budget and discuss how he's distributing his disposable income. If he doesn't have a budget—and the majority of the US population doesn't—ask if he'd be willing to create one with your help (and make sure you have your own budget). You can find a copy of a budget worksheet at the end of this book or online at www.prosperwell.com.

How He Feels about Estate Planning

Ask if he has a will or trust, health care directive, or a durable power of attorney. Find out as well if those documents are up-to-date. If he doesn't have either, ask why.

His Financial Past and Future

Before you can figure out where you are going together, you need to know where you have been as individuals.

If the very thought of discussing these questions gives you a migraine, consider meeting with a wealth advisor to help ease you through the process. If you'd rather tackle them yourself, find ways to make the talk less heavy. Cook one of your favorite meals together before you dive in, so you've got something comforting and fun to balance out the stress. Take breaks in the discussion to watch goofy YouTube videos or walk around the block together. Hold hands during the emotionally vulnerable parts so you feel grounded in each other. You can't avoid these topics, but you *can* find ways to make their discussion more palatable to you both!

Summary

The big, weighty talks that committed couples have tend to focus on topics other than money, but everyone should dig into financial matters together. If you're getting ready to take your relationship to the next level of commitment, carve out time to have the conversation about money. You will save yourselves heartache and become stronger as a couple for having done so.

Words of Wisdom

A great relationship doesn't happen because of the love you had in the beginning, but how well you continue building love until the end.
—Unknown

10

The Financially
Independent Woman

I was dating a new guy, and we had been on a few dates. He then invited me on a date to Mall of America, and my girlfriend got me super excited because she thought he must be taking me shopping. It was finally "my turn" since in the past I was always financially taking care of everything in my relationships.

We got to the mall, and we shopped around. He asked if there was anything I wanted to try on, and there was not anything I was interested in buying. We then proceeded to the Coach store because I was in the market for a new purse and wallet, and Coach is my go-to brand. I picked one out and brought it up to the counter. As I was doing so, he left the store to "go look at something else." Thankfully I was fully prepared to pay for the purse myself. We then went to another store, and I picked out a pair of shoes and paid for them—shoes I didn't even need. I was testing him to see if he invited me to actually take me shopping or if he was the one testing me to see if I expected him to pay for my things. Either way, I was not interested in him at that point. We eventually went to lunch, and I was shocked when he paid the whole check. It was an awkward and uncomfortable date that I still don't understand what the point of it was.

Cautious Carrie

***

The biggest mistake I see single women making is allowing themselves to become financially reliant on their partners. Unfortunately, I see them making this mistake *over and over again.*

It is perfectly fine to prefer a partner who outearns you, and it is totally reasonable to insist on dating men who can pull their own weight. I'm not saying that every single woman should be the breadwinner in her relationship or that agreeing to split financial burdens is flat-out lunacy. However, if you're older or divorced, you need to be in a position to cover all of your own expenses (plus those of your children) without any help. You need to be in a stable financial position with a solid plan in place before you even consider merging bank accounts with someone else. You need to be utterly and completely financially independent. Period.

And in this chapter, I'm going to tell you how to do that.

The Basics of Investing

Financial independence can take many forms, and it can be a pretty overwhelming concept to contemplate. To make things clearer and more comprehensible, I'm going to use a case study to walk you through the basics. The people in it are composites of clients and the details. Though fictional, they are 100 percent feasible for an ambitious single woman. Let's dig in!

Maya is a single woman who is looking to enter the dating world, but she knows that she needs to get her financial house in order first. Just like with dating, the first thing she needs to figure out are her goals. Where does she want to be financially? Does she want to retire when she's fifty or sixty-five? Does she want to be at the end of her life having joyfully spent every last dime—or would she prefer to give a substantial amount to her kids or charity? Does she want to be an aggressive investor—or is she naturally conservative? Acknowledging what kind of investor you are can help you set feasible and obtainable financial goals.

When you invest, you want to start with the basics. You want to put your money into three main categories: stocks, bonds, and cash. Once you have the basics, you can expand into alternatives and commodities such as gold, silver, real estate, hedge funds, etc. This is a lot like dating. You need to meet a variety of people to understand the scope of what's available. Doing so is both healthy and enriching. Wealth advisors lean on the concept of *diversification* because it can lead to overall financial health.

What is the difference between diversification and allocation? Asset allocation is an investment technique that diversifies a portfolio among equities, fixed income, and cash equivalents. The assumed level of risk for any investor is based on a number of factors, including risk tolerance, time horizon, and investment goals. Diversification, on the other hand, is taking your asset allocation and diversifying it among various asset *classes*.

Maya is a big fan of *dollar-cost averaging*, which means investing money every month into an account. Equal monetary amounts are regularly and periodically invested over a specific time period (such as $100 a month) into a particular investment or portfolio. Since the number of shares that can be bought for a fixed amount of money varies with stock price, dollar-cost averaging leads to more shares being purchased when their price is low and fewer when it's high. As a result, dollar-cost averaging lowers the total average cost per share of the investment, giving the investor a lower overall cost for the shares purchased over time. For example, let's say Maya put away $100 every month for twelve months. At the end of that year, she will have the average cost for the year versus just taking $1,200 and investing it on a single day at one price. Dollar-cost averaging is ideal for many investors because it's a lot easier to come up with $100 a month than a lump sum of $1,200 at one time.

Looking at the Long Term

When you buy an investment, you should know your long-term plan. What's your investing strategy? Are you buying stock with the intention of owning it forever? Are you buying the stock to make a 20 percent profit and then sell out completely? Will you take the 20 percent that you earned and put that money into another investment?

Also consider your backup plans and fail-safes. When investing in stocks, you can put a stop-loss in place to protect yourself. A stop-loss is an order placed with a wealth advisor to sell a security if it reaches a certain price. This tool is designed to limit an investor's loss on a position in a security. Although most investors associate a stop-loss order with a long position, it can also be used for a short position, in which case, the security would be *bought* if it trades above a defined price. This can be incredibly helpful if you realize you have made a bad investment and need to get out. Sometimes you buy an investment that seems wise in the moment, but as time goes on, it may not make sense for you to own it anymore. Diversification and asset allocation do not ensure a profit or protect against a loss. Keep in mind that there is no assurance that any strategy will ultimately be successful or profitable—or protect against loss.

Once you know your strategy and have an escape hatch or two in place, educate yourself on the types of investments you want to make. Be prepared to do some exploring and experimenting before you find your perfect balance of investments. Investing, like dating, is a long-term activity. You can't go on one date and know he or she is the one. Just like you can't buy one stock and decide that's all you need to do to save for retirement! When it comes to your money (and your relationships), you need to be willing to play the field to find an ideal fit.

Maya is committed to investing a little bit each month, but she wants to investigate all her options. There are lots of them: stocks, bonds, exchange-traded funds (ETFs), and mutual funds are among the most common, but there are many others. Let's cruise through the basics with Maya and see what sounds good.

Stocks, Bonds, and Beyond

We've all heard the term *stock* float around when people talk investment strategy, but just what is a stock? It's basically an ownership share in a corporation. Each share denotes partial ownership for a shareowner, stockholder, or shareholder of that company. Each person who owns stock basically owns a piece of the organization overall. Stocks are traded on exchanges all over the world, and their prices fluctuate daily.

You might have heard the term *blue chip stocks* used in reference to shares of large, well-established, consistently profitable companies. These stocks may also be called *large cap* or *large capital*, which reference the size of the company. If stocks were people, large caps would be older, more experienced, and potentially more stable types: Think Donald Trump, Bill Clinton, George Clooney, Halle Berry, Sharon Stone, or Demi Moore. Heavy-hitters with long careers. Large cap stocks are often considered to be safer, more conservative investments. You need to ask yourself if that is what you want in your portfolio.

If the very notion of a large cap bores you, look elsewhere. Maybe you want to put your money into an edgy IPO (initial public offering)? An IPO is the first sale of stock by a company to the public, which usually happens when a new but fast-growing company is looking to capitalize on its exponential success. These emerging companies can raise money by issuing either debt or equity to its new shareholders. If stocks were people, IPOs would be young, cutting-edge, risky but exciting in their trajectories: actress Margot Robbie, businesswoman Marissa Mayer, singer Bruno Mars, or model Gigi Hadid. Serious earners who are absolutely on fire but haven't been around very long. IPOs are definitely exciting, but they can also be risky. When Facebook went public, there was so much hype over the stock that prices plummeted right away. These companies are much less established, younger, and less experienced, which may make them more volatile, but also more fun.

If handpicking stocks on your own sounds daunting to you, you're not alone. New investors often start with mutual funds, which are basically groups of stocks or groups of bonds. They're investment vehicles made up of a pool of funds collected from many investors for the purpose of investing in securities such as stocks, bonds, money market instruments, and similar assets. Mutual funds are operated by money managers who invest the fund's capital and attempt to produce gains and income for the fund's investors. The appeal is that a professional is driving the train and—at least in theory—making informed decisions about when and what to buy and sell.

An ETF is an investment fund traded on stock exchanges, much like stocks. ETFs hold assets such as stocks, commodities, or bonds, and the fund is traded close to its net asset value over the course of the trading day. Most ETFs track an index, such as a stock index or bond index.

A bond is a debt investment in which an investor loans money to an entity that borrows the funds for a defined period of time at a fixed interest rate. Bonds are used by companies, municipalities, states, and US and foreign governments to finance a variety of projects and activities. They are considered some of the most stable investment vehicles. Although they don't earn much, they seldom lose value.

I strongly recommend having a little bit of your whole portfolio diversified and not just investing in one thing. This does not mean holding five different accounts with five different advisors! It means having one account with a number of different investments that, in combination, give you a diversified mix. However, there is a point at which you can become too diversified and have money spread in too many places. A good advisor will be able to steer you away from this path.

Calculating and Considering Net Worth

You don't just need to be smart with your money—you need to be happy with where you are financially. If you are not satisfied, look at what you can change to get yourself back on the path to happiness. You might be surprised to hear this, but understanding your net worth can be a big part of that personal financial recalibration.

When I ask someone their net worth, most of the time, their eyes glaze over—and I get that deer-in-the-headlights look. I promise the concept is simpler than it sounds. Your net worth is simply a snapshot of everything you own minus anything you owe. It's a statement of what you are worth.

Don't know yours? Here's what you do: Take a sheet of paper and write down everything you own and put a dollar value beside it. Add everything up, and you've got your total assets. Then write down everything that you owe, total it up, and you've got your total liabilities. Take your total assets and subtract your total liabilities to find your total net worth.

Let's use Maya as an example. She's a single, forty-three-year-old woman, living by herself in a house. She works as a consultant making $110,000 a year.

Maya's Net Worth Statement

Real Estate

House Tax Value	$300,000
Total House	**$300,000**

Investments

Insured Money Market Account (1% interest)	$20,000
Investment Account	$12,000
Total Non-Retirement	**$32,000**

Roth IRA	$18,000
401(k) Current Job	$25,000
401(k) Prior Job	$60,000
IRA Rollover	$200,000
Total Retirement	**$303,000**

Other Assets

Car	$45,000
Jet Ski	$5,000
Total Other Assets	**$50,000**

Total Home	$300,000
Total Non-Retirement	$32,000
Total Retirement	$303,000
Total Other Assets	$50,000
Grand Total Assets	**$685,000**

Liabilities

Credit Card #1 (17% Interest)	($3,000)
Credit Card #2 (10% Interest)	($5,000)
Auto Loan (0% Interest)	($20,000)
30-Year Mortgage (6% Interest)	($150,000)
Total Liabilities	**($178,000)**

Total Net Worth (Assets Minus Liabilities)	**$507,000**

Maya could make a few small changes to her finances that would have a huge impact on her stability today, thereby positioning her to get where she wants to be in the future. Just like slipping on a brand-new red dress that highlights her best assets, which could help Maya catch the eye of her ideal mate—and change the direction of her dating as well as her life forever.

Here's how I'd advise Maya to change her fiscal life for the better:

Most wealth advisors—myself included—will tell you to have six to twelve months of liquid money set aside for emergencies, ideally in an insured money market account, but it doesn't pay to have a lot of money sitting in an account earning 1 percent interest when you have debt that is costing you 10 percent or more. Maya has credit cards that are charging her interest rates of more than 10 percent, which means she should immediately take $8,000 from her liquid money market account and pay off her two credit cards. It doesn't make sense to keep $8,000 in an account where you are only earning 1 percent while simultaneously paying out more than 10 percent to deal with a balance on your credit card. There's no getting ahead in that scenario. Get rid of bad debt immediately, even if it decreases your liquid assets.

Maya is paying a 6 percent interest rate on a $150,000 home loan for thirty years. This gives her a monthly payment of principal and interest of $899.33 per month. At this rate, she will pay a total of $323,757.28 for her house over the course of thirty years, so I'd strongly suggest she refinance. To do this, she has two options: She can keep the thirty-year mortgage and just refinance to lower her monthly payment—or she can reduce her mortgage from thirty years to fifteen. In the first scenario, if she secured a 4.5 percent interest rate that would lower her monthly payments to $760.03 per month, reduce her total to $273,610.07, and save her $50,147.21. In the second scenario, reducing the length of her mortgage helps her maximize savings over time. Switching to a fifteen-year mortgage will also give her access to a reduced interest rate, though it will increase her monthly payment. Say she refinances to fifteen years at a rate of 4 percent. This will give her a monthly payment of $1,109.53 and a total payout of $199,715.74 over the life of the loan. By paying off her loan quicker at a lower interest rate, she would save herself $124,041.54.

Assuming she can afford this monthly payment every month, this is by far her most efficient option.

Next Maya should focus on maxing out the retirement plans available to her. She's forty-three years old and easily able to put $19,000 a year into her 401(k) plus an additional $6,000 into her Roth IRA (a special retirement account that is funded with post-tax income). It is especially important that Maya contributes to her 401(k) plan since all the money she puts into it is pretax and deductible for her. This contribution to her 401(k) lowers her taxable income, so the first advantage is she will pay less in taxes. Since she's putting money directly into a retirement account in her name, she makes less income and pays fewer taxes on the income that is counted. Also, there are income limits on Roth IRAs, and only people below a certain earning threshold are eligible to contribute. So, the second advantage of contributing to the 401(k) is that it allows Maya to stay below the income threshold, allowing her to continue to contribute to her Roth IRA. The best way to invest in a Roth IRA is by doing so automatically every month. By doing this, you truly are paying yourself first. Your wealth advisor can automatically pull from your savings or checking account and deposit the contribution into your Roth IRA at your desired frequency. Since there is no set rate of return in a Roth IRA, how much you earn is determined by how you (or your wealth advisors) invest the money. In a Roth IRA, you can be as conservative or as aggressive as you want to be. You could buy individual stocks, or you could buy bonds, real estate, or any other type of specialty investment. You can basically invest in anything via an IRA. The Roth IRA does not give you a tax benefit today because the money you put into the account is comprised of after-tax dollars. However, that means when you go to withdraw in retirement, the money you take out is tax-free. (Be aware that, withdrawals before age 59.5 could be subject to a 10 percent IRS penalty. This is meant to be a retirement account, so tapping it before you're of legal retirement age has its drawbacks.) Unless certain criteria are met, Roth IRA owners must be 59.5 or older and have held the IRA for five years before tax-free withdrawals are permitted.

Finally, Maya should move the money from her old 401(k) into her IRA Rollover. A rollover is the movement of funds between two retirement plans (such as from a 401(k) plan to an IRA). Anytime you have an old 401(k), 403(b), or 457 plan, you generally want to consolidate and roll them into one IRA Rollover. Rolling the plan into an IRA gives the owner the ability to choose from a much wider array of investments. IRAs allow virtually any type of investment to be placed within them, with a small handful of exceptions. The investment options in many 401(k) plans are fairly limited and may not be particularly competitive with what is available elsewhere. Other advantages include lower fees in an IRA, more control over your choices, and consolidation.

> Which of the changes that were suggested
> for Maya reminded you of changes you need
> to make to your own finances?

In addition to rolling over your 401(k), there are other options. Here is a brief look at all your options. For additional information and what is suitable for your particular situation, please consult with your wealth advisor.

Leave money in your former employer's plan, if permitted.

Pro: May like the investments offered in the plan and may not have a fee for leaving it in the plan. Not a taxable event.

Roll over the assets to your new employer's plan. If one is available and it is permitted.

Pro: Keeping it all together and larger sum of money working for you, not a taxable event.

Con: Not all employer plans accept rollovers.

Roll over to an IRA.

> Pro: Likely more investment options, not a taxable event, consolidating accounts and locations.

> Con: Usually fee involved, potential termination fees.

Cash out the account.

> Con: A taxable event, loss of investing potential. Costly for young individuals under 59.5. There is a penalty of 10 percent in addition to income taxes.

You should consider all of your available options and the applicable fees and features of each option before moving your retirement assets.

Let's say Maya takes my advice and makes these four changes. This is what her new balance sheet would look like:

Maya's Net Worth Statement

Real Estate
House Tax Value	$300,000
Total House	**$300,000**

Investments
Insured Money Market Account (1% interest)	$12,000
Investment Account	$12,000
Total Non-Retirement	**$24,000**

Roth IRA	$18,000
401(k)Current Job	$25,000
IRA Rollover	$260,000
Total Retirement	**$303,000**

Other Assets
Car	$45,000
Jet Ski	$5,000
Total Other Assets	**$50,000**

Total Home	$300,000
Total Non-Retirement	$24,000
Total Retirement	$303,000
Total Other Assets	$50,000
Grand Total Assets	**$677,000**

Liabilities
Auto Loan (0% Interest)	($20,000)
15-Year Mortgage (4% Interest)	($150,000)
Total Liabilities	**($170,000)**

Total Net Worth (Assets minus Liabilities)	**$507,000**

Making these small changes would not have increased Maya's net worth overnight, but it should have lowered her interest rates and her monthly payments. This, in turn, should increase her cash flow and her ability to save more money monthly, which in the long term, should increase her net worth. Her finances should be simpler, smarter, and leaner. The more you can simplify your financial statement and how you handle your finances, the easier your allocation and financial life should be to manage.

Refining Your Finances

Now that Maya made some changes to her cash flow that should eventually raise her net worth, let's see how her investments should be allocated and suggest some further adjustments:

Maya should take any monies that are in CDs within her Roth IRA and put into more aggressive investments. Remember that within a Roth IRA, you can have stocks, bonds, CDs, or any other types of investment vehicles. So why should Maya move any IRA money that's currently locked up in CDs? For two important reasons. First, the Roth IRA is generally going to be the last account you use in your retirement years. Second, whatever you earn in the Roth IRA should be tax-free as long as you take it out during retirement. Therefore, Maya should not keep any of the money in her Roth IRA in a CD that only pays 1 percent. She should take that money out of the CD and change it to a more aggressive investment within the Roth IRA, such as a small cap or mid cap mutual fund, ETF, or even a stock, depending on how aggressive or conservative she wants to be and how much risk she can handle.

With her other retirement investments, Maya should diversify with equities (which are stocks). Maya should want to have her money in small, medium, and large companies and also consider alternative investments. The important thing is to have a portfolio that is allocated correctly so that Maya wouldn't lose sleep at night. When Maya rolled her old 401(k), she kept that money *in cash* in her IRA Rollover, which means, in the long term, she's actually losing money because of inflation, which is when prices increase but the value of money goes down or stays flat. She should make sure that the cash in her IRA Rollover gets invested in a diversified portfolio.

The investment profile is hypothetical, and the asset allocations are presented only as examples and are not intended as investment advice. Actual investor results will vary as investing involves risk, fluctuation, and the possibility of loss.

With non-retirement assets, she should keep some money liquid and accessible. She has $12,000 liquid and her goal is to have six to twelve months of income set aside in liquid money. Since Maya makes $110,000 a year, her goal is to have at least $50,000 in an insured money market account. This account is for emergencies or the things that happen in life that you don't expect such as a medical cost, job loss, etc. This way, if Maya were to lose her job, she could meet her expenses every month until she found a new job and replaced her income. Emergency funds should be in an insured minimum account so they are available for you whenever you need them.

Your Finances, Shared Finances

Now that Maya has her net worth in order and her allocation suited to fit her moderately aggressive investing style, she's ready to focus on her love life. She's investing wisely, and she's in a position to handle all of her expenses and still save for retirement. She's a financially independent woman, and she's ready to meet her match!

Maya has taken time to reflect and created a list of what she wants in a partner so she can hit the dating scene running. Maya wants someone who is:

- a nonsmoker
- comfortable budgeting with her
- a travel lover
- taller than her
- earning more than $80,000 per year
- confident
- a great communicator
- close with his family
- not afraid of being emotionally intimate

Maya spends a few months dating, and she eventually meets Miles. They hit it off and fall head over heels in love. Within a year, they are engaged and planning a beautiful wedding. However, before they do that, they realize they need to discuss their finances and make sure they are on the same page.

Miles is forty-five and wants to retire at fifty-five. Both he and Maya make about $100,000 a year. Maya has $303,000 saved toward her retirement, and Miles has $550,000. Each can have their own wealth advisor and their own plan, but it's important that Maya and Miles come together to make sure that their plans are working together at full speed.

The investment profile is hypothetical, and the asset allocations are presented only as examples and are not intended as investment advice. Actual investor results will vary as investing involves risk, fluctuation, and the possibility of loss.

Think of the analogy of a canoe. Maya and Miles are paddling down the river toward their destination, but all of a sudden, Miles looks back and realizes one of the paddles is dragging behind them and slowing them down. This can easily happen if communication breaks down around finances. For instance, if Maya's employer offers a 401(k) match, and she isn't taking advantage of it, that is like a paddle slowing them down as they attempt to achieve their financial goals.

Maya and Miles have a money date and decide to keep their finances separate but each contribute to a "fun account." They will each will put $500 per month into this account to use for their dates and activities. They plan to keep the rest of their finances separate for now since Miles owns his own home as well, and they're not yet ready to merge households.

Let's take a look at how their two sets of finances compare.

Maya's Net Worth Statement

Real Estate

House Tax Value	$300,000
Total Home	**$300,000**

Investments

Insured Money Market Account (1% interest)	$12,000
Investment Account	$12,000
Total Non-Retirement	**$24,000**

Roth IRA	$18,000
401(k) (Current Job)	$25,000
IRA Rollover	$260,000
Total Retirement	**$303,000**

Other Assets

Car	$45,000
Jet Ski	$5,000
Total Other Assets	**$50,000**

Total Home	$300,000
Total Non-Retirement	$24,000
Total Retirement	$303,000
Total Other Assets	$50,000
Grand Total Assets	**$677,000**

Liabilities

Auto Loan (0% Interest)	($20,000)
15-Year Mortgage (4% Interest)	($150,000)
Total Liabilities	**($170,000)**

Total Net Worth (Assets Minus Liabilities)	**$507,000**

Miles's Net Worth Statement

Real Estate

House Tax Value	$500,000
Total Home	**$500,000**

Investments

Insured Money Market Account (1% interest)	$1,000
Total Non-Retirement	**$1,000**

Roth IRA	$100,000
401(k) (Current Job)	$50,000
IRA Rollover	$400,000
Total Retirement	**$550,000**

Other Assets

Car	$51,000
Total Other Assets	**$51,000**

Total Home	$500,000
Total Non-Retirement	$1,000
Total Retirement	$550,000
Total Other Assets	$51,000
Grand Total Assets	**$1,102,000**

Liabilities

Auto Loan	$0.00
Mortgage	$0.00
Total Liabilities	**$0.00**

Total Net Worth (Assets minus Liabilities)	**$1,102,000**

Although Miles has no debt and a greater net worth, it does not necessarily mean he is in a better financial state than Maya. Is he using his assets wisely? Is his money distributed as it should be? He may look better on paper in some ways, but an astute wealth advisor would suggest many changes. Having walked through Maya's finances, can you guess what they might be?

- He needs more liquid money.
- He should make sure the money in his retirement accounts is invested correctly.
- Although life without monthly housing costs can be freeing, having a mortgage might actually benefit Miles, especially when it comes to taxes or if he was considering launching a new business.

Don't revel in being the partner with the more impressive net worth. Instead, find ways to become a united financial team with shared goals and a solid savings plan. In the end, you need to decide jointly what is best for you, your money, and your heart.

However, you also need to maintain your financial independence! Lean into the goals you create together, but don't be ashamed of wanting to keep a pool of money just for yourself in case things go sideways. It's not the best idea to merge your money with someone in a worse financial state than yourself. Your relationship should be one plus one equals one thousand and not one plus one equals negative one thousand.

Financial independence is freedom, and freedom is power. Once you've carved out true financial independence for yourself, you get to hang onto that power—and no one can take it away from you.

Summary

It's absolutely essential to get your own finances in great shape before you partner up. Never fall into the trap of believing the right man will save you from a money mess. Create a plan (with advice from a wealth advisor), stick to it, and put yourself on the road to financial independence. Then, and only then, will you be ready to merge your life with someone else's.

> ### *Words of Wisdom*
>
> *As a woman you are better off in life earning your own money. You couldn't prevent your husband from leaving you or taking another wife, but you could have some of your dignity if you didn't have to beg him for financial support.*
> —Ayaan Hirsi Ali

11

Money, Marriage, and Maturity

I was out on a first date with a seemingly nice professional man, and our dinner was coming to an end. He offered to buy. I thanked him and then offered to pay the next time. I could tell he would be open to a second date, so I wanted to let him know that we were on the same page. When we got up to leave, the bartender came out from behind the bar and approached us. He was a distinguished-looking older gentleman with a lovely accent and a friendly smile who'd given us impeccable service, just as he had when I'd visited this establishment in the past. He asked us how the food and drinks were, and then he asked about how we felt his service had been. He had been fantastic, so my date and I both said so. Then he asked again, and in a more serious tone, "Are you sure that you had good service?" When we said yes again, he asked, "Then why did you leave me a seven-dollar tip on a hundred-dollar bill?" My date kind of shrugged and started walking toward the door. I took out a twenty and left it on the bar with a quiet apology to the bartender. Clearly, we were not on the same page when it came to money and values. We didn't end up going on that second date.

Sabrina the Self-Sufficient

***

By now, you should know that you'll cope with a variety of money issues at every stage of your relationship, and you understand that discussing them all is essential. It's so easy to push money matters to the back burner as your love grows and your relationship progresses. You may think, *Oh, we've covered all that. Why bring it all up again?*

As a couple, it is important that you talk about your finances *regularly,* so you are both on the same page when it comes to budgeting, saving, and investing. Don't fall into the trap of leaving one of you to handle the finances, while the other has no clue about what is going on. Even if it is easier to put one person in charge of the bills and investments, you still want to make sure you're both involved and aware of your situation. When you both know balances and details, it curtails the resentments that arise if one of you spends more money than the other.

Try to make regular money dates to talk about your finances. They might not be as much fun as steak dinners or nights at the movies, but they'll do more for the health and longevity of your relationship in the long run. You can also make them fun if you work toward achieving your goals together and focus on putting your money toward expenses that improve your quality of life and move you toward your long-term goals.

If you are single right now and not seeing anyone on a regular basis, make a money date with yourself! Otherwise, set an appointment with your wealth advisor to go over your plan. It is important to know where your finances are right now so that you can plan for where you want to be in the future.

Money Health, Relationship Health

Most of us know what a healthy, happy relationship looks like. Even if many of our own love affairs have been a little on the dysfunctional side, we can still recognize the thriving relationships around us. What are the essential elements of a successful relationship?

- Communication: You *must* feel comfortable talking things out with your partner. Even issues that are complex, shameful, or overwhelming.
- Commitment: Both people need to be equally committed to the relationship, whether it's a casual bond or a lifelong marriage. When there's imbalance here, it causes strife elsewhere.

- Humor: You need to be able to laugh at yourself and laugh with your partner. This may seem minor, but it can literally make or break a relationship!
- Trust: Without trust, you have nothing. Period.
- Honesty: Being honest with your partner is very important. You should think of yourselves as a team—and never keep things from each other.
- Gratitude: Relationship studies show that couples who frequently and openly express their appreciation for one another have a better shot at long-term happiness.

All six of these factors should apply to your money relationship too. You should communicate often and openly about money fluctuations and concerns. Be committed to the same financial goals. Handle hiccups with good humor. Trust each other with cash, credit, and investments. Always be honest about your individual and joint finances. Express gratitude. Maintaining a successful relationship means being successful with money.

It's important to acknowledge that your money priorities may shift over time. Things that were nonnegotiable when you were single may not fit into your shared life. For instance, a man I've known for many years always invested in season tickets for several local teams while he was a single guy. Once he started seeing a woman exclusively, the games provided lots of fun "date nights," and made many of her sports-fan friends envious, but after they got married, the cost of those tickets became a point of contention. With new shared costs, the hefty expense of maintaining multiple season tickets seemed frivolous, and attending tons of games lost some of its appeal. In the end, they canceled the subscriptions.

On a related note, you'll save yourself countless headaches if you address any recurring sources of financial tension directly. A former colleague who has been married to his wife for forty-two years told me a story about remodeling the kitchen in their shared house that perfectly illustrates this point. My colleague is a mutual fund executive. As a result, he tends to be pretty thrifty, but his wife, a pediatric nurse, has more of a "you-only-live-once" attitude toward spending. As they were working their way through the remodel, she was insistent that they install a fancy Viking range and oven that would set them back $18,000. They fought over it for weeks, and she finally overrode him. In the end, he said he was fine with the decision because she was so passionate about it … and because he knew that his naturally conservative nature could balance out her more liberal spending habits.

As our relationships grow and mature, our money changes and our values change. We need to make sure that our partner's values are in line with our own values at all times, and that means communicating about money. Not just once, but with healthy regularity.

> Communication, commitment, humor, trust, honesty, and gratitude are the six key elements of a healthy relationship. Which of those needs the most work in *your* relationship?

Moving Toward Marriage and Considering Prenups

Let's say you are in the enviable position of having found your ideal match. You've dated through all four seasons, met his family, spent months (or years) getting to know each other, and decided you want to spend the rest of your life together. Before you make that lifelong commitment, you need to know where you stand financially and how you fit together. You must identify any issues that need resolution *before* you get hitched.

I believe that you should be together for two years at the very least before getting engaged. I remember when a couple I knew got serious quickly and started discussing the possibility of getting married. Then they began to dig into money matters, and he discovered she had a fairly large debt load. He told her he wouldn't marry her until she had paid off her credit card balances. She was a little surprised by such a frank statement, but she saw how important financial responsibility was to him—and how he wanted that to carry over into their relationship. He helped her pay off all the credit card debt, and they kept it paid off. They've been married sixteen years now and have never carried a balance on a credit card.

Before you say yes to a ring and a shared life together, make sure you've done the following:

- Met with a wealth advisor together: There's a lot you can figure out on your own, but it's best to consult a pro on the overarching issues. A wealth advisor can help facilitate how you'll handle your money and your investments as a couple.
- Shared each other's credit scores and reports: Don't forget to also discuss what they mean.
- Developed a budget together: Make a plan that works for you both.
- Created a plan for your finances: Will bank accounts or investment accounts be shared, separate, or a mixture? How will you handle shared expenses?
- Discussed your net worth statements: Be sure to also develop a plan to merge and grow your net worth together

Any preliminary discussions about values, money, and goals may lead to mulling over the pros and cons of creating a prenuptial agreement. It is also called an antenuptial agreement or premarital agreement and is commonly abbreviated as prenup or prenupt. A prenuptial agreement is a contract entered into prior to marriage or civil union. The content of the agreement can vary widely, but it commonly includes provisions for division of property and spousal support in the event of divorce or dissolution of the marriage. Prenups may also include terms for the forfeiture of assets as a result of divorce on the grounds of adultery or specific conditions for guardianship of children.

Speaking of adultery, it's worth noting that marital infidelity is more common than many people think, and it is something that happens even in happy marriages. The journal *Sex Roles* conducted a study of married men who had cheated on their spouses and found that 56 percent considered their marriages to be happy and healthy. Men aren't always the bad guys.

A recent General Social Survey showed that men and women cheat in almost equal numbers in their early years. After age forty-nine, the gap widens, and more men cheat. Other research has indicated that women are actually more likely to cheat if they feel unhappy or ungratified in their marriage. Food for thought if you were thinking, "Oh, well, *we* certainly don't need a prenup!"

When I asked my friends, colleagues, and clients to share their views on whether prenups were necessary, respondents shared a mix of opinions.

Many said yes, stating that a prenup forces a frank discussion about financial expectations at the outset of marriage. Some of those same people said that divorce turns humans into animals and pointed out that settling on some key financial and custody terms ahead of time is a necessary evil.

On the other side, many said no because they felt that entering a marriage was like starting a business. It required a lot of work and commitment by all parties. They felt creating a prenup was equivalent to saying you expected things to eventually end in divorce. This group valued trust and teamwork over extreme caution.

There was also a group that couldn't say yes or no definitively, feeling that the necessity of a prenup would depend on a number of factors, including children from a previous marriage, imbalance of assets held by one party, stage of life, and age.

I have watched numerous marriages and partnerships fall apart over the years. Some have crashed and burned, while others were dissolved civilly. Regardless of how messy or amicable these separations appeared from the outside, I know they were all emotionally exhausting. What I've learned from my own experience and from watching friends and clients cope with separations and divorces, is that certain circumstances make forethought and prudence absolutely necessary. If you have young children, a growing business, or substantial assets to protect, a prenup is a precautionary measure that will help you enter into new relationships with less anxiety and more peace of mind. You don't expect to need your life vest while on a flight, but you sure do learn where it is and how to use it just in case. Doing so does not increase the odds of your plane landing in the Pacific Ocean.

For more information on creating a solid, equitable prenup, get a copy of *Prenuptial Agreements: How to Write a Fair and Lasting Contract* by Katherine Stoner and Shae Irving. You can also reach out to my office for an attorney referral.

Creating a Plan for Marriage or Cohabitation

If you're engaged and knee-deep in wedding planning, I'll assume you've already had several money discussions and learned about each other's financial status, but have you created a marriage plan? If you are a business owner, you'd never dive into a new endeavor without a business plan. Why not apply that same level of mindful preparation to your personal life? After all, marriage *is* a contract and has many similarities to running a business.

Before you get married, you should explore your individual and shared values, goals, dreams, and desires. A marriage plan can capture some of those ideas and visions, but it can also work like a financial plan. It can state what you want to achieve together, how you prefer to communicate, and milestones you'd like to reach by certain dates. Just as a financial plan outlines and captures your goals, a marriage plan can solidify your mutual desires and keep you on the same page over time.

How do you create a marriage plan? First, block off some time for you and your partner to have a planning session free of distractions. You'll need about half a day. Discuss the following ten topics and take detailed notes:

1. **Reminisce**. Talk about how you met and what first attracted you to each other. Set the scene by reliving the excitement of those early days.
2. **Create a marriage/family vision statement**. Craft a statement that describes how you want your family to operate. Keep it short and sweet (no more than five sentences). Try to steer clear of don'ts and won'ts. Instead, focus on what you want to do, be, and achieve.
3. **Plan regular date nights**. Commit to dating each other throughout your marriage. Ideally, you should spend one-on-one time at least once per week. Nothing extinguishes a flame like lack of intimate interaction, but spending time together can quickly fall to the wayside if both spouses are busy with work or kids. Pick a date night early—and stick to it!
4. **Choose a marriage book to read together**. Read it during the lead-up to the wedding—or read one chapter each week for the next few months. This will give you some outside perspective on your existing relationship, tips for improving it, and a framework for discussing what does and doesn't work.
5. **Evaluate your health and wellness**. Do you need to find time to exercise? Are you on the same page about food and nutrition?

This may seem minor, but it will become more and more relevant as you age together. It also impacts how you shop, cook for each other, and divide up your free time. (If one of you runs marathons and the other is a couch potato, that *will* become an issue.) Discuss your priorities and agree on how you'll manage and monitor your health.

6. **Create a rough budget (or revisit your current one).** You may not be able to foresee all of your shared expenses, but you can create a working budget as a starting point. At the back of this book and at www.prosperwell.com, you'll find a worksheet that will help you build a budget from scratch. Remember, arguments about money are one of the greatest causes of strife in a relationship. Cut them off at the pass by working out a fair and rational budget together.

7. **Chat about children.** Are you on the same page about having (or not having) children? Do you agree on how many you want? If you already have kids, are you and your spouse-to-be on the same page about discipline and rewards? What do you want to teach your kids?

8. **Set partnership goals.** How can you improve yourself as a partner? What changes would you like your partner to work on? Be gentle and diplomatic, but also take this time to dig into any issues around communication, sharing tasks, priorities, family, and other interpersonal issues that need finessing.

9. **Explore ambitions, dreams, and desires.** What do you want to do? Where do you want to go? What needs to happen in order to accomplish these dreams? What does your life look like during the next year? Five years? What do you want to achieve as an individual and as a couple? Examine both—and outline rough action plans.

10. **Plan your next marriage retreat.** Just as money needs frequent discussion, so does your relationship. Schedule a multi-hour discussion at least once per year, ideally somewhere outside your home. Make it into a weekend getaway. Hop on a plane, drive to a bed-and-breakfast, or just install yourselves in your favorite coffee shop for hours. Make sure you're somewhere new and stimulating,

able to put phones and tech away, and be ready to get truly focused. Get your next retreat on the calendar ASAP.

Your marriage retreats will focus on both emotional and financial matters, but be aware that they provide a great opportunity to revisit your credit reports and check for any discrepancies. Before the retreat, you can go to www.annualcreditreport.com and get one copy from each of the three credit bureaus. As I mentioned in chapter 9, your credit score is one of the most important numbers in your life. When you marry someone, you are attaching yourself to that person financially. If your ideal match has a credit score of 600, and you have a score of 810, you need to acknowledge that your score could drop when you get married. Therefore, should you really get married? If your partner's score continues to drop, that will affect you too. It is vital to evaluate and discuss credit scores on a regular basis.

This sample marriage plan can serve as a guide, but feel free to add more topics! If there are any issues or concerns that you want to address in your unique plan, by all means include them.

Getting on the same page with your values isn't just wise—it's imperative. If you don't get into full alignment early on, it could lead to disaster. For instance, let's pretend you are in a relationship with someone who doesn't care about paying bills on time. It doesn't bother him one bit if he makes late payments or is charged late fees. You, on the other hand, have the personality of a recovering perfectionist, always pay your bills on time, and can't imagine shelling out for pointless late fees. Given your divergent money values, you need to decide how you'll handle bill payments—and examine if it might be a deal-breaker. A devil-may-care attitude toward financial obligations is often an indicator of deeper and more serious money issues, so unearthing something like this could give you early warning. Think seriously about proceeding with your engagement if you and your fiancé clash on something fundamental.

Money Matters for Homemakers

Much of what we've discussed so far assumes you both work and both intend to keep working, but what if one of you hopes to stay home with the kids or to care for the home (or multiple homes) and pets? This adds a new dimension to money discussions, and it will have a huge impact on your marriage plan, budgeting decisions, and any prenup agreements you might enter.

In decades past, it was more common for married women *not to work* than it was to hold jobs outside the home. Those statistics have shifted. With more women in the traditional workforce, many people have come to devalue the labor, stress, and skill required to keep a home and family in great shape. Women (or men) who stay home are described as women (or men) who "don't work," despite the fact that they may work all day every day to keep the house clean, the pantry stocked, the kids shuttled to various activities, the pets healthy, and themselves sane! Wives and husbands who don't work outside the home are excused from contributing money for bills or household expenses, but they aren't directly compensated for their labor and dedication.

Today, we see more *men* opting to stay home with the kids while their wives pursue careers and more same-sex couples in which only one person works outside the home. Being the stay-at-home spouse is no longer defined by gender. We may be tempted to put people in boxes to streamline our understanding of the world, but when we generalize and label people with stereotypes, we limit both them and ourselves.

As our society has gradually become more open-minded, some people have suggested that partners and spouses who stay home should be compensated monetarily for their contributions. How would dynamics shift if the spouse who earned a paycheck paid the spouse who ran the home?

A new trend has emerged that sees wives being paid by their husbands for the work they do at home (and vice versa if gender roles are swapped). Most aren't issued a weekly check or allowance, but instead are given "bonuses." The spouse who does the "job" of working in the home receives a percentage of the paycheck from the spouse who works at the office. This creates guilt-free spending money for the significant other who worked hard inside the home, making it possible for the other partner to work outside the home to the best of his or her ability. Some couples have chosen to base this rate or amount upon the spouse's performance at work—especially if that spouse works on commission or runs a business—as well as how well the other spouse manages the home, kids, budget, etc.

I like the groundwork this lays for couples and families and the way it frames concepts of work and compensation. I think you should set goals as a family, and if you achieve those goals, you should be rewarded. Don't think of it as his salary and his bonus or her salary and her bonus. When you are in a true partnership, it's all jointly *yours*. You have money coming in as a family and going out as a family. You make spending and reward decisions based upon your money goals as a family.

A couple I worked with as clients chose to swap traditional gender roles, and it worked beautifully for them. He stayed at home with the kids, allowing her to build up her company and focus on her career. He took care of the house, finances, and kids, and she focused on work. He really went the extra mile as a "house husband." She told me when she'd had a tough day at work, she'd come home—and he'd have dinner ready and a bath drawn for her! They both felt that this breakdown of labor and duties felt right and made sense. She worked, and they both spent time with their kids instead of both working and hiring out the childcare and housework.

Common Money Mistakes

Bad money management can be very costly and significant for couples. Poorly researched decisions can lead to catastrophic choices that hurt you both. Some common money mistakes made between couples include:

1. Living together without a shared lease and/or cohabitation agreement. If only one name is listed, you leave yourself open to being thrown out on the street at a moment's notice if you break up.
2. Spending beyond your means (especially toward the beginning of the relationship). Make sure that how you act at the start is how you plan to act throughout.
3. Not creating and sticking to a budget. If you don't have a budget, how can you stick to one? A budget gets you closer to reaching your financial goals.
4. Not having the money talk before marriage. Couples who don't have a money talk may ultimately be surprised by the costly impact that one partner's low credit score has on the interest rate for their shared mortgage and other loans. You'll also be more likely to fight about budgeting, saving, spending, and investing.

5. Not treating each other's retirement accounts as a single portfolio. Take a big-picture view of your investments and establish an over-all asset allocation that's appropriate.

6. Claiming Social Security benefits too early. Yes, you can start claiming at sixty-two, and early retirement can be tempting, but your benefit will be permanently reduced by a fraction of a percent for each month that you claim before your full retirement age.

7. Not deciding how to pay for any costs associated with children. If you care for his children along with yours, who should pay for what? Kids are expensive, and the costs can become contentious. (If you already have kids and are dating, I would recommend accepting that your kids are your kids, and you are 100 percent responsible for them.)

8. Believing that taking an expensive vacation will fix your relation-ship. Not a chance. Save that money, stay home, and work on your problems together.

9. Not respecting each other's money values—or not knowing them at all!

10. Letting minor fights about money get out of hand. Even if you have regular money dates and amazing communication, you will still have disagreements about money. That's totally normal. Just make sure that an issue that begins as a tiff doesn't fester into deep-seeded resentment.

All of these mistakes can be easily avoided, and all of them can be canceled out if you maintain open and honest communication about money.

Relationships are all about give and take. Just as you want to be loved and respected, you want to treat someone you care about with love and respect. You want them to feel appreciated and valued—just like your money. Over the years, I have advised my clients to open their wallets and look at their cash. Yes, the real hard currency. Today, more and more people use their debit and credit cards for everything, but most of us still carry a few bills.

Therefore, open your wallet and look at your cash. Looking at your wallet will give you a fresh perspective. What do you see? Is your money in order? Do you have the one-dollar bills, then the fives, tens, etc. in order?

Are some bills backwards? Are some upside down? If your wallet is nice and organized, you most likely know how much money is in there. You treat your money with respect, which means it will treat you with respect.

Similarly, if you treat your partner with respect, he will treat you with respect. If you know his financial situation and he knows yours, you'll be in sync in other areas of your shared life. If you appreciate and value him, it's hard to go wrong.

Summary

Make it a priority to jointly develop and reassess your family financial plan throughout your relationship to ensure you are both on track to meet your goals. Create a marriage plan together, schedule regular marriage retreats, and check in on money matters frequently.

> ### Words of Wisdom
>
> *The right man for you will move mountains to be with you—he won't hide behind them.*
> —Mandy Hale

12

Navigating the World of Blended Families

I was just divorced from my oldest daughter's father and was set up on a date with a guy who seemed nice and interested in me. We had talked on the phone for the past few weeks, and he had invited me to meet him for dinner. At the restaurant, he asked me about my job, my life, and my family. I explained to him that I was a single mother, and to make ends meet, I recently moved back in with my own mother to get caught up on bills and help me finish my recovery from cancer. At the time of the date, I had been in remission for five months.

As we got more into our conversation, he smiled and asked, "Would you every consider giving up custody of your daughter to her father so that you could have a meaningful relationship with someone?"

I couldn't believe he said that and told him that we are a package deal and that should never be asked of anyone. He said, "I don't feel that I should be tied down to a lady with a kid." When the server came to take out order, I ordered the most expensive thing on the menu, excused myself to go to the restroom, and left the restaurant.

A few days later, he sent me a bill in the mail for my dinner. I returned it to him with a note: "I feel that you made an ass of yourself requesting I give up my child to have a meaningful relationship with a man. A real man would accept the child or children in the woman's life that he wishes to get to know and have a meaningful relationship with."

I never heard from him again!

Mama Mindy

***

Today's modern family looks different than it did in the 1950s. No longer is the average family measured by the yardstick of a mom, a dad, two kids, and Fido. We have gay marriage and blended families—modern-day families have changed the landscape of what a family looks like.

On television, there is more diversity in commercials, and families are represented in different forms much more than ever before. This is growth. With growth comes growing pains. Embrace them as opportunities to learn and improve.

This new landscape and frontier is somewhat uncharted. Blended families have been around for decades, but the way we interact and grow as blended families has evolved. How we communicate as blended families or divorced couples has changed. These days, there are apps and websites to help two households manage children going back and forth.

We practically have a new language centered around the world of blended families. Back in the 1970s, we didn't hear terms like "co-parenting," "parenting time," "parent on duty," or "parallel parenting." We have evolved when it comes to what a family looks like today.

There was a time where divorce meant you lived with your mother and saw your dad on the weekends. Today, it's more common for fathers to share fifty-fifty in parenting time. This has also changed how child support is handled in courts. Mothers paying child support or spousal maintenance was once unheard of. That is not the case today.

If you are a single parent or a single who is dating a parent, there are key points you need to discuss and address with the person you are considering marrying or living with. When two adults fall in love and build a life together, they need only consider themselves for the most part. When parents fall in love, they have other individuals to consider. The success or failure in a relationship has a much larger effect when children are involved. Children tie two people together for a lifetime—whether they choose to have it that way or not. "Till death do us part" takes on a whole new meaning when you bring children into the world together.

You now may be dealing with your partner's ex, much more than if they didn't have children together. Your partner or you may have an obligation of child support or spousal maintenance. Relationships have many more moving parts with children.

Not Just Money Issues

Don't make the mistake of assuming it will all work out and that you and your partner are on the same page when it comes to money and your blended family. By now, you should have a good understanding of each other's financial health as well as a plan for how you are going to grow your wealth together.

What happens when birthdays or holidays roll around where gifts are needed for the children? Do you both cover the cost? Does one of you? Is the cost kept equal from child to child regardless of whose child it is?

These are not issues that are just about money. We each have a past, and that past can show up to play in the present. I knew a woman who was a brilliant, successful attorney and mother. She fell in love with and married a man who also had children and was very financially successful.

Being an attorney and a financially independent woman, she took steps to protect herself and him as well from a financial perspective. She thought she had covered all of her basis, and then one of her kids turned sixteen and needed a car. She wanted to give the child an extra car she and her husband seldom used. Her husband was not supportive of this, even though he had purchased brand-new vehicles for his own children when they turned sixteen. It had nothing to do with having enough money. They had the money to provide a new car for the child if they wanted to. These issues have more to do with not having an agreement in place ahead of time.

This is a point I cannot stress enough. While it's impossible to discuss and plan for every possible financial scenario a blended family could face, it's vital that you discuss and come to agreements on the main issues.

- Who pays for gifts for the children?
- How will you handle cars, cell phones, and other larger purchases?
- What about college?

- How will child support or spousal maintenance payments affect your finances?
- Will your spouse or you contribute to medical expenses?
- How will you handle vacations or dinners out as a family?

There is no one right answer for these questions because everyone's situation is different. The way to circumvent upsets later is to discuss these scenarios before you are cohabitating or married. It might be uncomfortable to think or talk about, but you are saving yourselves resentment and heartache in the long run.

The key is to establish an agreement between you. It's easy to think you can coast along on love alone, but you need to be realistic. If you have been married before, you know till death do you part is more of a concept than a reality for many.

When it comes to your financial health, you must deal in facts and not emotions. The more you can discuss with your partner and come to agreements on before you are married or living together, the better off you will be.

When you were working on our Partner List, kids or no kids should be on that list. If you feel strongly that you do not want to raise someone else's children, then do not date someone with children. There is nothing wrong with not wanting to take on someone else's children or even to not want children of your own. The first part of this book is centered around discovering who you are. If you falter from who you are, you build a relationship on a shaky foundation. When children are involved, it is even more important that the foundation be strong.

Set the Right Precedents

As a parent, it isn't always possible to be fair in the eyes of your children. Children often perceive anything not going their way as unfair. Contrary to the beliefs of a child, your primary job as a parent is not catering to the whims of your children.

How many times have you witnessed two kids fighting over who gets the bigger scoop of ice cream? Have you ever seen siblings count how many presents are under the Christmas tree, checking to see it here are an equal amount? This happens with siblings who share the same parents.

Imagine what it is like for siblings who don't share the same parents but are now living as a family? They may be more sensitive to perceived inequalities. If their stepbrother gets a new car at sixteen, they may expect or being severely disappointed if they don't get a car at sixteen.

Precedents set before you moved in together or got married can't be undone. What you can control is how you handle things moving forward. Have a discussion about what is important to you as a parent when it comes to providing for your child. Just because you can afford a new car for your sixteen-year-old, it doesn't mean you should buy a new car.

Managing the expectations of your children will create a smoother road. There will never be exact equality. Someone will always get the bigger ice cream scoop. Someone will have to take the middle seat in the back of the car at times.

What matters is that you and your significant other acknowledge, discuss, and come to agreements on how you are going to handle these big-picture items. Do that—and you will have won more than half of the battle. Resentment is a cancer when it comes to relationships. You take preventive measures with your health. Take them for your financial health and the well-being of your family as well.

> Learn to separate emotion from reality when it comes to your children's—or their children's—needs. At the end of the day, what matters is where you are going as a family and not where you have been.

Benefits of a Blended Family

Blended families have a wonderful opportunity to foster compassion and selflessness in their children and each other. They say family is not who you share blood with but who you would give your blood for. Many of us are closer to friends than we are members of our blood families.

It's important to have honest, open, age-appropriate conversations with the children involved in a blended family. Set that precedent right off the bat. Children are incredibly resilient. They do better when they know what to expect or know what you expect from them.

They may not always remember what you say, but your actions stick with them. Lead by example. If you want them to speak to each other and you with respect and kindness, you had better be doing the same. This is a benefit because you may find yourself trying harder to be patient with children who are not biologically yours. It is similar to the way you put your best foot forward while dating their parent.

That should not stop. When you are dating and move into more of a serious relationship, you should treat your partner with the same kindness and respect you showed at the start. Relationships start to go downhill when we start to take each other for granted and let up on the politeness of a new relationship.

If you wouldn't use the bathroom in front of a date on the first date, why would you do so nine months or two years in to your relationship? Please, thank you, and other considerate gestures are the kindling that stokes the fire of romance.

With a blended family, you don't have the history with the child or children of your partner that he or she does. That means you don't know them as well, but it also means they don't know your buttons, which kids love to push. You have a fresh start at your relationship with that child. Get to know them for who they are separate from their parent, while showing them who you are as an individual as well.

Something else is to consider is what happens when and if your ex moves on and creates a blended family. That is not something that is within your control, but it will affect you and your children.

What is in your control is how you communicate with our ex and his or her new partner. His new blended family is an opportunity for you to rise above the emotions and ties of the past. Recognize that you may have unexpected feelings when there is someone other than you or your children's other parent parenting them.

Your child or children may have a stepparent. My strong advice is to learn to work with and respect that person. This is someone who has made a choice to love and care for your children. They did not play a hand in creating those kids, but they can influence them in the long run for the better. This is one more person who will love your children. This is one more person to put their shoulder to the wheel when it comes to parenting these little people into adulthood. This person is choosing to do this. They don't have to.

Ideally, your kids fall madly in love with their new stepparent. This is a good thing. Use this as an opportunity to model acceptance, kindness, and respect. I've seen too many situations where moms resent the new mother figure in their children's lives for no reason other than their own insecurities and jealousy. Yes, it happens with dads too, but I've seen it more with moms.

Don't be that mom or dad who tries to get between her kids and the new stepparent. Your children will always love you, and they will always know you are their mother or father. A stepparent is an additional parent and not a replacement. Thinking your children might love him or her more is like thinking you could love one of your children more than the other. At times, we like one of them more than the other, but we always love them with the same gusto.

Summary

Blended families are an opportunity for growth on everyone's part. Involving children makes it even more vital for you to discuss and come to agreements on key, big-picture financial matters that affect everyone.

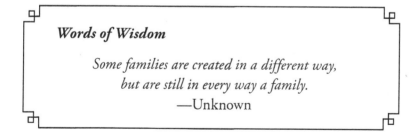

Words of Wisdom

Some families are created in a different way,
but are still in every way a family.
—Unknown

13

Love Yourself First

When I met and fell in love with my husband, I moved into his house, joined him in his hobbies, and simply lost myself. As time went on, I put my own needs, desires, and dreams on the back burner. He was my world. Eventually feelings of resentment began to creep in. I realized that, in loving him, I stopped loving myself.

Empty Emily

***

Finding love can feel like a race. Society expects you to partner up and settle down by a certain age, and if you haven't, things can get awkward. Society expects you to quickly get engaged and succumb to the pressure to get married before you really, truly know your partner.

Finding love can feel like a competition. When all of your friends are married or dating, and you're the lone single girl, you may wonder what they've got that you lack.

Finding love can feel like a scavenger hunt. It takes a lot of energy and a lot of cunning to sort through all the mismatches until you find your ideal fit.

In my opinion, finding love is much less about other people and much more about you. If I've learned anything in my years of postdivorce dating, it's that you've got to love yourself first.

Loving yourself means being completely in control of your own finances. It means knowing where you've been, where you are, and where you're going. It means having a smart financial plan and sticking to it. Money can't buy you happiness, but it can buy you something close to it: peace of mind. Never forget that. When you partner with someone, remember that they should complement your money goals and never impede them.

Loving yourself means protecting yourself. It means knowing exactly who you're meeting for a date and having an escape plan in case he turns out to be a deadbeat. It means sharing details about your finances, your identity, and your personal information with great caution. It means using your common sense and being aware of the current social environment. And when you find your ideal mate, he will respect and uphold the boundaries you've set.

Loving yourself means communicating your needs, wants, and ambitions. It means getting over your fears and talking openly about money. It means finding ways to share costs that feel fair to everyone. When you're in a committed relationship, it means making money dates, ensuring you share money values, and getting help if you're fighting over money.

Loving yourself means respecting yourself. It means not sending him nude photos before you discuss net worth. It means not being a gold digger. It means not confusing money or gifts or material things with sincere emotional commitment. It means not expecting him to read your mind and getting mad when he can't. It means not compromising your core values or pretending to be someone you're not just to please him.

Most of all, it means making yourself whole before you try to partner with someone else. A colleague once used this great analogy: If you're hurt, lost, or scared, you're like Pac-Man. There's a wedge-shaped chunk missing from you. You may try to find a partner who can fill that missing chunk, but it just won't work. If he's already whole, none of him will fit. If he's hurt too, he'll have a wedge missing—but he still can't fit snugly into your empty spot. You've both got to be whole. You need to feel complete as an individual to go through life side by side instead of trying to plug up each other's empty spaces.

In all my years as a wealth advisor, I've learned a lot about love and money. I've met women who seemed totally put together on the surface but were drowning in debt or painfully lonely. I've met women who felt trapped in their marriages and then watched them blossom after a liberating divorce. I've met women who are so dazzled by the rich men they've chosen to date that they can't see how shallow or rude or heartless these guys truly are.

My office is a safe space, and I'm always honored to see that my clients feel free to speak frankly about their lives and worries and hopes and dreams. They've given me an education, a glimpse into how varied human life can be. They've shown me that love takes many forms, and it shows up only when you're truly ready to receive it. They've shown me that sometimes love ends, but our resilience rises up. I may have written this book myself, but they all contributed. Without their candor and insight, I could never have compiled this compendium of advice about matters of the heart and of the pocketbook.

I hope what I've shared here has been helpful, enlightening, and enjoyable. If you're young and dating right now, I hope you'll refer back to later chapters once you're married or committed. If you're older and just getting back into the dating game, I hope my suggestions gave you a surge of hope and excitement about this new phase of life you're entering.

No matter who you are, if you take just one thing away from reading this book, I hope it's this: Finding love isn't about searching the world for Mr. Right. It's about searching yourself until you've become Ms. Right—and letting Mr. Right find you.

Resources and Further Reading

Prosperwell Financial
www.prosperwell.com

Prosperwell Financial provides personalized wealth management advice to effectively guide you through every stage of life. Our advisors help plan your way toward true financial happiness, including financial retirement planning, college education savings, estate planning, asset management, insurance, and financial divorce planning. Founded by wealth advisor and Certified Divorce Financial Analyst Nicole Middendorf, Prosperwell Financial serves individuals and executives all across the United States.

Mint
www.mint.com

This comprehensive website brings together everything from balances and bills to your credit score and more. It's your financial life—in one place that's easy to understand. Mint is totally free and easy to use, and the site connects to almost every US financial institution connected to the Internet. In just minutes, you'll see where your money is going and get ideas for how to stretch it farther.

QuickBooks
www.quickbooks.com

QuickBooks is an accounting software package geared mainly toward small and medium-sized businesses, but it is also incredibly useful for individuals. You can use it to accept business payments, manage and pay bills, administer payroll functions, track tax-related information, and more.

The 5 Love Languages: The Secret to Love that Lasts
Gary Chapman

In this #1 *New York Times* bestseller, you'll discover a communication template that has transformed millions of relationships worldwide. Whether your relationship is flourishing or failing, Dr. Gary Chapman's proven approach to showing and receiving love will help you experience deeper and richer levels of intimacy with your partner. The book even includes a couple's assessment, so you can discover your love own language, as well as that of your loved one.

The End of Men: And the Rise of Women
Hanna Rosin

Written by *Atlantic* senior editor and "Invisibilia" podcast founder Hanna Rosin, this book examines a paradigm shift currently turning the gender norms of American society upside down. Rosin explores these changing norms across several settings, from the bedroom to the jail cell, and teases out the highs and lows experienced by women attempting to shoulder the breadwinner and housekeeper roles simultaneously.

Lean In: Women, Work, and the Will to Lead
Sheryl Sandberg

Sheryl Sandberg—Facebook COO, ranked eighth on Fortune's list of the 50 Most Powerful Women in Business—wrote this provocative, inspiring book about women and power. She fuses humorous personal anecdotes, singular lessons on confidence and leadership, and practical advice for women based on research, data, her own experiences, and the experiences of other women of all ages. Through *Lean In*, Sandberg urges women to take risks and seek new challenges, to find work that they love, and to remain passionately engaged with it at the highest levels throughout their lives.

The Nice Girl Syndrome: Stop Being Manipulated and Abused—and Start Standing Up for Yourself
Beverly Engel

Are you too nice for your own good? Do family members manipulate you? Do coworkers take advantage of you? If this sounds familiar, read *The Nice Girl Syndrome.* In this breakthrough guide, renowned author and therapist Beverly Engel, who has helped thousands of women recognize and leave emotionally abusive relationships, can show you how to take control of your life and take care of yourself.

Sedona Method: How to Get Rid of Your Emotional Baggage and Live the Life You Want
Hale Dwoskin

The Sedona Method offers a simple yet highly effective way to eliminate the painful emotions and limiting thoughts that sabotage your success, happiness, and well-being. Master the releasing process and learn how to achieve your goals, improve your relationships, and experience the life you've always wanted. Modern personal development techniques—such as affirmations, positive thinking, and NLP—have focused on changing our thinking and reprogramming the mind. With practical techniques and enlightening true stories, this book shows you how to manifest what you want while learning to be at ease with what you already have.

The Self-Love Experiment: Fifteen Principles for Becoming More Kind, Compassionate, and Accepting of Yourself
Shannon Kaiser

Too many people seem to believe that they are not allowed to put themselves first or go after their own dreams out of fear of being selfish or sacrificing others' needs. *The Self-Love Experiment* addresses this problem head-on. Whether you want to achieve weight loss, land your dream job, find your soul mate, or get out of debt, it all comes back to self-love and accepting yourself first. Kaiser learned the secrets to loving herself, finding purpose, and living a passion-filled life after recovering from eating disorders, drug addictions, corporate burnout, and depression. Now a successful life coach, she guides her readers toward lasting self-love.

Women Who Love Too Much: When You Keep Wishing and Hoping He'll Change
Robin Norwood

Do you find yourself attracted again and again to troubled, distant, moody men—while "nice guys" seem boring? Do you obsess over men who are emotionally unavailable, addicted to work, hobbies, alcohol, or other women? Do you neglect your friends and your own interests to be immediately available to him? Do you feel empty without him, even though being with him is torment? Robin Norwood's groundbreaking work will enable you to recognize the roots of your destructive patterns of relating and provide you with a step-by-step guide to a more rewarding way of living and loving.

Your Live It List™

What makes you happy? What do you want to do in life? Where do you want to travel? These are all things that make up your Live It List™. The Live It List™ was designed to help keep track of all the things you want to do while living your life to the fullest.

What is on your Live It List™? Would you see more stage plays? Go back to school? Try skydiving? Take a dance class? What activities do you want to bring into your life to help you appreciate it every day, and understand your true self better?

List at least 10 of them here:

1. _____

2. _____

3. _____

4. _____

5. _____

6. _____

7. _____

8. _____

9. _____

10. _____

Budget Worksheet

Net Income: _____

Living Expenses

Mortgage/Rent: _____

Second Mortgage: _____

Home Insurance: _____

Property Taxes: _____

Assessment: _____

Condo Fees: _____

Dining Out: _____

Lunch at Work: _____

Groceries: _____

Bedding/Linens: _____

Pet Expenses: _____

Postage: _____

Home-Maintenance Expenses

Furniture: _____

Interior Repairs: _____

Home Supplies: _____

House Cleaning: _____

Decorating: _____

Lawn Mowing: _____

Landscaper: _____

Snow Blowing: _____

Furnace Filters: _____

Garbage: _____

Security System: _____

Water Softener Salt: _____

Tree Trimming: _____

Spring/Fall Cleanup: _____

House Painting: _____

Gardening: _____

Plumber: _____

Room Maintenance: _____

Irrigation: _____

Pest Maintenance: _____

Water System: _____

Personal Expenses

Clothing: _____

Hosiery: _____

Shoes: _____

Haircuts: _____

Beauty Salon: _____

Jewelry: _____

Beauty Supplies: _____

Massage: _____

Manicure/Pedicure: _____

Alterations/Repairs: _____

Dry Cleaning: _____

Spousal Maintenance: _____

Utilities

Electricity: _____

Gas: _____

Water: _____

Phone: _____

Cable TV: _____

Cell Phone: _____

Long Distance: _____

Pager: _____

Voicemail: _____

DSL/Internet: _____

Sewer/Septic: _____

Firewood: _____

Transportation

Car Loan/Lease: _____

Gas: _____

Car Insurance: _____

Vehicle Tabs: _____

Car Washes: _____

Oil Changes: _____

Parking: _____

Maintenance: _____

Repairs: _____

Bus Pass: _____

Bikes: _____

Car Savings: _____

Medical

Doctor Visits: _____

Health Insurance: _____

Eyeglasses/contacts: _____

Dental: _____

Medications: _____

Medicare Supplements: _____

LTC Insurance: _____

Life Insurance: _____

Disability Insurance: _____

Vitamins: _____

Health Savings Account: _____

Recreation

Hobbies: _____

Relaxation: _____

Sport Activities: _____

Vacation: _____

Theater: _____

Sports Events: _____

Movies: _____

Entertainment: _____

Home Entertaining: _____

Boat Expenses: _____

Boat Insurance: _____

Watercraft Expenses: _____

Watercraft Insurance: _____

Pool Expenses: _____

Memberships

AAA: _____

Golf Club: _____

Country Club: . _____

Sam's Club: _____

Costco: _____

Golf League: _____

Bowling League: _____

Other Leagues: _____

Health/Fitness Club: _____

Fish/Hunt Licenses: _____

Union Dues: _____

Debit/Credit Cards

_____   _____
_____   _____
_____   _____
_____   _____

Savings

401(k)/457/403b: _____
Roth/Traditional IRA: _____
Deferred Comp: _____
Liquid Money: _____
VUL Insurance: _____
Annuity: _____
Spending Money: _____
529/Ed IRA/UTMA: _____

Miscellaneous

School Expenses: _____
Paper/Copies: _____
Laundry: _____
Cards/Gifts: _____
Donations: _____
Travel: _____
Cigarettes: _____
Alcohol: _____
Magazines: _____
Books: _____
Accountant Fees: _____
Financial Fees: _____
Attorney Fees: _____

Income Taxes: _____

Safe-Deposit Box: _____

Newspapers: _____

Kids' Expenses _____

Clothing: _____

Shoes: _____

Food: _____

Transportation: _____

School Expenses: _____

Cell Phone: _____

Lunch Money: _____

Personal Supplies: _____

Haircuts: _____

Babysitter: _____

Nanny: _____

Child Support: _____

Day Care: _____

Diapers: _____

Diaper Service: _____

Medical: _____

Summer Camp: _____

Activities: _____

Lessons: _____

Parenting Consultant: _____

Supervision: _____

Allowance: _____

Kids Expenses:

Personal Expenses:

Total Expenses: _____

Short/Over: _____

Assembling Your Financial Team

CPA _____
- What is their expertise? _____
- What is their role? _____
- How do you know they are doing their role? _____

Wealth Advisor_____
- What is their expertise? _____
- What is their role? _____
- How do you know they are doing their role? _____

Estate Attorney_____
- What is their expertise? _____
- What is their role? _____
- How do you know they are doing their role? _____

Business Attorney _____
- What is their expertise? _____
- What is their role? _____
- How do you know they are doing their role? _____

Banker _____
- What is their expertise? _____
- What is their role? _____
- How do you know they are doing their role? _____

Property and Casualty Insurance Agent _____
- What is their expertise? _____
- What is their role? _____
- How do you know they are doing their role? _____

Life/Business Coach _____
- What is their expertise? _____
- What is their role? _____
- How do you know they are doing their role? _____

Financial Checklist for Before, During, and After Divorce

Complete the checklist items that apply to you and your situation. Take time to consult with the appropriate professionals for assistance and guidance. This checklist does not represent the order in which to address these issues; it is only a preliminary guide and is not intended to be a comprehensive list of things to consider.

Before Your Divorce

Document your team of consultants (include their names and phone numbers)
Family Law Attorney: _____
Accountant: _____
Certified Divorce Financial Analyst: _____
Business Attorney: _____
Banker: _____
Wealth Advisor: _____
Insurance Agent: _____
Other: _____

Financial
- Fill out our Divorce Information Sheet.
- Gather copies of your investment statements.
- Gather copies of your last three years of tax returns.
- Fill out a Monthly Budget Worksheet.
- Open a checking and saving account in your own name.
- Review your beneficiaries on all accounts.

During Your Divorce

Legal

- Consider establishing a trust for the benefit of your children.

Financial

- Determine divorce settlement.
- Review ownership and custodial responsibility of children's accounts.
- Fill out new account paperwork.
- If you need a QDRO (Qualified Domestic Relations Order), have an attorney start the document.
- Prepare accounts to transfer to just your name.

Life and Health Insurance

- Purchase or change life insurance that would be required by your divorce decree to cover child support or spousal maintenance.
- Review policies on your life to ensure that they are meeting your current needs.
- Apply for coverage through your employer or apply for individual health coverage, or continue COBRA benefits through your ex-spouse's employer (for up to three years).
- Review your policies to ensure that they are meeting your current needs.
- Consider long-term care or disability coverage (if you don't currently have coverage).

Social Security/Veteran Benefits

- Contact the Social Security Administration for eligibility information at www.ssa.gov.
- Confirm your benefit amount if you are currently collecting Social Security.
- Contact the VA about veteran's benefits (www.vba.va.gov.).

Taxes

- Meet with your tax professional to determine your new tax status and strategies.

After Your Divorce

Legal

- Make sure you have several copies of your divorce decree.
- Retitle assets, including real estate and automobiles.
- Make name-change notifications.
- Establish a new power of attorney for yourself.
- Name a new health care agent within your health care directive.
- Create a new will and establish appropriate trusts.

Financial

- Close and distribute all joint assets according to your divorce decree.
- Complete transfer of assets.
- Look over your asset allocation and adjust as needed.
- Refinance your mortgage.
- Do a Quit Claim Deed (once appropriate).
- Set up accounts monthly to invest.

Life Insurance

- Make beneficiary changes.

Other considerations

_____

_____

_____

Your Partner List

A partner list is a list of traits and qualities that you feel are important in a partner to have. It may be physical attributes, personality characteristics, that they share similar hobbies, have special talents, etc.

Take some time right now to start your very own Partner List. Don't worry about putting items in order of importance, just brainstorm and jot down anything that comes to mind. You can revise and add more later on.

1. _____

2. _____

3. _____

4. _____

5. _____

6. _____

7. _____

8. _____

9. _____

10. _____

Money Personalities

It is good to know your money personality so that you understand your habits and understand your areas to work on. It is also important to identify and know your significant others money personality.

The Saver – You are great at saving money and putting it away. Because of this you find it difficult to spend money on things that you enjoy. You focus too much on cutting costs and sacrificing in order to build your savings and security.

The Spender – You are great at getting yourself into debt. You love life and are willing to spend money on things to help you enjoy it. You are typically the one with numerous maxed out credit cards and other loans with little savings.

The Avoider – You ignore your money. It is perhaps because it is complicated to deal with or perhaps you fear it. You don't know how much you spend or how much you are saving at any given time.

If you see yourself in any of these categories, make a plan to utilize your strengths and balance out your weaknesses.

What is your money personality? _____

_____

What is your partner's money personality? _____

_____

The What If's in Life

I believe smart financial planning is a continuous process, and the main focus should be examining the "what if's" of your life. Some of them include the following things happening in our lives. A great exercise is to sit down together and answer these questions. The more you discuss different scenarios that can happen the more prepared you will be and in return less stressed. It will also aide the strength in your relationship.

1.   What if I lose my job?

                _____

                _____

2.   What if my partner loses their job?

                _____

                _____

3.   What if my partner dies?

                _____

                _____

4.   What if I die?

                _____

                _____

5.   What if my partner dies?

                _____

                _____

6.   What if my parents die?

                _____

                _____

7. What if I get married?

_____

_____

8. What if I get pregnant?

_____

_____

9. What if I get in a car accident?

_____

_____

10. What if my partner gets in a car accident?

_____

_____

11. What if my/our child is hurt?

_____

_____

12. What if I have a medical emergency?

_____

_____

13. What if my partner has a medical emergency?

_____

_____

14. What if I become disabled?

_____

_____

15. What if my partner becomes disabled?

_____

_____

16. What if my/our house burns down?

_____

_____

17. What if I lose my/our business?

_____

_____

18. What if I get a promotion?

_____

_____

19. What if my partner gets a promotion?

_____

_____

20. What if I win the lottery?

_____

_____

21. What if my partner wins the lottery?

_____

_____

Money Questions

To fully protect yourself and your finances, you need to know the following things about anyone you choose to date seriously and exclusively:

Question	Me	You
Personal/Work Background		
Financial History (ever filed for bankruptcy?)		
Financial Stability (how much in savings, debt, etc)		
How daring are you with your investments?		
Are you on track to retire?		
How will you meet your cash flow needs in the future?		
Are you a saver or a spender?		
Beliefs and Values regarding money		
Favorite Money Memory		

Questions to Ask

As you prepare to discuss money matters, here are some questions to help break the ice and get you started.

Money Values

1.   If you could change one thing about your financial situation, what would it be?

Me:

_____

_____

You:

_____

_____

2.   How much is in your savings account? Investment account?

Me:

_____

_____

You:

_____

_____

3.   Is there anything you are saving money for right now?

Me:

_____

_____

You:

_____

_____

4.   Where do you want to be in one year? Five years? Ten years? Twenty years?

Me:

_____

_____

You:

_____

_____

5.   Can we discuss setting a dollar amount which neither of us would spend without consulting the other?

Me:

_____

_____

You:

_____

_____

6.   How did your family discuss or handle money matters?

Me:

_____

_____

You:

_____

_____

7. Are you a millionaire? Do you want to be? Why or why not?

Me:

_____

_____

You:

_____

_____

8. Does money make you happy? Why or why not?

Me:

_____

_____

You:

_____

_____

9. How will we keep things equal? What if you spend $100 and I spend $1,000 on an anniversary gift? Will this matter?

Me:

_____

_____

You:

_____

_____

10. How much money do you donate each year? Which organizations, people, or things top your donation list? Why are they important to you?

Me:

_____

_____

You:

_____

_____

11. Do you love your job?

Me:

_____

_____

You:

_____

_____

12. Would you keep working the same job even if you didn't get paid?

Me:

_____

_____

You:

_____

_____

13. What are the next two items on your Live It List™, and how will you pay for them?

Me:

_____

_____

You:

_____

_____

14. If we were to get married, would we sign prenups?

Me:

_____

_____

You:

_____

_____

15.   If you won $10,000, what would you do with your winnings?

Me:

_____

_____

You:

_____

_____

16.   If you were given two years left to live, what if any changes would you make in your life?

Me:

_____

_____

You:

_____

_____

Cash Flow

1.   If an unexpected expense of $10,000 came up, how would you cover that expense?

Me:

_____

_____

You:

_____

_____

2. How much do you have in your checking account? Do you balance
your checking account? Why or why not?

Me:

_____

_____

You:

_____

_____

3. How much income do you make? Are you W-2 or 1099?

Me:

_____

_____

You:

_____

_____

4. Can you make it month-to-month on your current income? If not,
what are you doing about it?

Me:

_____

_____

You:

_____

_____

5. What do you spend too much on each month?

Me:

_____

_____

6.   Do you have a budget? If you don't, would you be willing to create one?

Me:

_____

_____

You:

_____

_____

7.   How much money on average do you have left after your monthly expenses?

Me:

_____

_____

You:

_____

_____

Retirement

1.   How much do you have saved for retirement?

Me:

_____

_____

You:

_____

_____

2. How much do you save for retirement each month, and where do
    you put it?

    Me:

    _____

    _____

    You:

    _____

    _____

3. At what age do you want to retire? How much income do you want
    to have available on a monthly basis when you stop working?

    Me:

    _____

    _____

    You:

    _____

    _____

4. Do you have life insurance? If so, how much? What kind?

    Me:

    _____

    _____

    You:

    _____

    _____

5. Do you have a will? A trust? What do they say?

Me:

_____

_____

You:

_____

_____

6. Do you have a Roth IRA? Why or why not? Do you qualify to add to the Roth IRA?

Me:

_____

_____

You:

_____

_____

7. Do you have company stock? Is it more than 5% of your net worth? Why or why not?

Me:

_____

_____

You:

_____

_____

8. Do you think you are going to inherit money?

Me:

_____

_____

You:

_____

_____

9.   If you could afford to retire tomorrow, would you?

Me:

_____

_____

You:

_____

_____

Assets

1.   How much is your home worth? How much do you owe on your mortgage? What is the interest rate? How many years remain on your loan?

Me:

_____

_____

You:

_____

_____

2.   How is the value of your automobile? Do you have a loan on it? What is the interest rate? How much time is left on your loan?

Me:

_____

_____

You:

_____

_____

3.   What other assets do you have? What other assets do you want to accumulate?

Me:

_____

_____

You:

_____

_____

4.   Do you own a business? If so, how is it set up? What are your plans for your company? What is your day-to-day like?

Me:

_____

_____

You:

_____

_____

5.   If you don't own a business, would you ever want to start one?

Me:

_____

_____

You:

_____

_____

6. What is your favorite asset?

Me:

_____

_____

You:

_____

_____

7. What is the next asset you want to buy? How? When?

Me:

_____

_____

You:

_____

_____

Children

1. Do you have college accounts set up for your kids? If so, what type and how much?

Me:

_____

_____

You:

_____

_____

2. If we merge our lives together, will we share our kids' expenses? Including college?

Me:

_____

_____

You:

_____

_____

3.   How do you teach your kids about money?

Me:

_____

_____

You:

_____

_____

4.   Do you give your kids an allowance? How much? What do they use it for? Do they do any chores or meet any academic standards before they receive it?

Me:

_____

_____

You:

_____

_____

5.   Do you have a family 401(k)? Why or why not?

Me:

_____

_____

You:

_____

_____

6. What is one thing you've learned about money that you wish you'd known as a kid?

    Me:

    _____

    _____

    You:

    _____

    _____

7. Have you done a "wants vs. needs" chart with your kids?

    Me:

    _____

    _____

    You:

    _____

    _____

8. When do you pay for things for your kids? When do you make them pay for them?

    Me:

    _____

    _____

    You:

    _____

    _____

Net Worth

1.   What is your net worth? List all your assets and liabilities.

Me:

_____

_____

You:

_____

_____

2.   Did your parents talk to you about money?

Me:

_____

_____

You:

_____

_____

3.   If you won $1,000,000 in the lottery, what would you do with it?

Me:

_____

_____

You:

_____

_____

4.   Do you spend time with people who have a greater net worth than you? Why or why not?

Me:

_____

You:

_____

_____

5.   Are you taking steps to increase your net worth?

Me:

_____

_____

You:

_____

_____

Credit

1.   What is your credit score?

Me:

_____

_____

You:

_____

_____

2.   Do you have credit card debt? If not, when was it last paid off?

Me:

_____

_____

You:

_____

_____

3.   When was the last time you were late on paying a bill? Why?

      Me:

      _____

      _____

      You:

      _____

      _____

4.   Do you have any bad debt? If so, what is your plan to get rid of it?

      Me:

      _____

      _____

      You:

      _____

      _____

5.   What are your thoughts and feelings about debt?

      Me:

      _____

      _____

      You:

      _____

      _____

Goals

1. Where do you want to be in one year?

   Me:

   _____

   _____

   You:

   _____

   _____

2. Where do you want to be in five years?

   Me:

   _____

   _____

   You:

   _____

   _____

3. Where do you want to be in ten years?

   Me:

   _____

   _____

   You:

   _____

   _____

4. Where do you want to be in 20 years?

    Me:

    _____

    _____

    You:

    _____

    _____

5. What is the one thing you will start doing today to get you to your goal?

    Me:

    _____

    _____

    You:

    _____

    _____

Disclosures

Prosperwell Financial is not a registered broker/dealer and is independent of Raymond James Financial Services, Inc. Securities offered through Raymond James Financial Services, Inc., member FINRA/SIPC. Investment advisory services offered through Raymond James Financial Services Advisors, Inc.

The information contained in this book does not purport to be a complete description of the securities, markets, or developments referred to in this material. The information has been obtained from sources considered to be reliable, but we do not guarantee that the foregoing material is accurate or complete. Any information is not a complete summary or statement of all available data necessary for making an investment decision and does not constitute a recommendation. Any opinions are those of Nicole Middendorf, and not necessarily those of Raymond James. Expressions of opinion are as of this date and are subject to change without notice. There is no guarantee that these statements, opinions, or forecasts provided herein will prove to be correct. Expressions of opinion are as of the initial book publishing date and are subject to change without notice.

Raymond James Financial Services, Inc. is not responsible for the consequences of any particular transaction or investment decision based on the content of this book. All financial, retirement, and estate planning should be individualized as each person's situation is unique.

This information is not intended as a solicitation or an offer to buy or sell any security referred to herein. Keep in mind that there is no assurance that the recommendations or strategies listed in the book will ultimately be successful or profitable nor protect against a loss. Investing involves risk, and you may incur a profit or loss regardless of strategy selected. There may also be the potential for missed growth opportunities that may occur after the sale of an investment. Recommendations, specific investments, or strategies discussed may not be suitable for all investors. Past performance may not be indicative of future results. Raymond James does not provide tax or legal services. You should discuss any tax or legal matters with the appropriate professional.